CROSSWAYS

4
SECTION

UNITS 31–40

The Postexilic Period and Judaism

Fourth Edition

Harry Wendt

CROSSWAYS
INTERNATIONAL
Minneapolis, MN

CROSSWAYS®—SECTION 4
was developed and written by
Harry Wendt, Minneapolis, MN

Illustrations by
Knarelle Beard, Adelaide, South Australia

The Bible text in this publication is from the New Revised Standard Version of the Bible,
copyright 1989 by the Division of Christian Education of the National Council of
Churches of Christ in the United States of America and used by permission.

CROSSWAYS®—SECTION 4
is published and distributed by
CROSSWAYS INTERNATIONAL
7930 Computer Avenue South
Minneapolis, MN 55435
www.crossways.org

Printed in China

Nihil Obstat: Ms. Catherine Cory, Ph. D.
February 24, 2014

Imprimatur: The Most Reverend John C. Nienstedt, STD
March 31, 2014

Ecclesiastical approval is a declaration that a book or
pamphlet is considered to be free from doctrinal or
moral error. It is not implied that those who have
granted the ecclesiastical approval agree with the
contents, opinions, or statements expressed.

ISBN 978-1-891245-21-3

Fourth Edition
10   9   8   7   6   5   4   3

We at Crossways International (CI) are delighted that you are about to undertake a study of the entire sweep of the Old and New Testaments using our materials as your guide. May your journey be fruitful and rewarding, and draw you ever closer to the mind, manner, and meaning of Jesus, the Servant-Messiah.

CI is more than a publisher of Christian education and Bible study materials. We also offer hands-on training in the use of our materials, and we make our materials available to special ministries and missions all around the world. We would be happy to partner with you in *any way* that might help you to share the Good News of God's Kingdom with the people you reach.

The courses of Crossways International have been translated into dozens of languages and are used by all major Christian denominations in numerous countries around the world. We have trained tens of thousands of pastors, teachers, and lay-people to teach the Bible with joy and passion.

WHAT DISTINGUISHES CROSSWAYS INTERNATIONAL?

1 A Panoramic View of Scripture

CI's courses examine the meaning of the Bible by digging into the *complete story* that runs through it—from *Genesis to Revelation*. We believe you cannot fully grasp the enormity and profundity of Jesus the Messiah's mind and message without understanding what preceded Him and set the stage for His ministry and mission.

2 Visual Learning

All of CI's teaching materials make extensive use of specially designed *color graphics* to help people better understand and remember the written material. These make it easier to share God's Good News.

3 Focus on Jesus, the Servant-King

We are not about biblical study merely for study's sake. The core of every CI course is *Jesus*, the *King who washed feet*—the Messiah who invites us to follow Him by loving and serving others— as He did. These courses help to *transform hearts and lives*.

4 Tools for Faith Development

CI offers *survey courses of increasing depth* that lead people through the entire story of the Bible—plus *short courses* on specific biblical topics, such as Jesus' parables, Christian stewardship, prayer, the Passion and the Christmas stories.

5 Workshop Training for Teachers & Laity

For those interested in *revitalizing their ministries* using CI's courses, we offer workshops that train attendees, step-by-step, how to do it. We also offer workshops for lay-people who are eager to boost their biblical literacy and steep themselves in Scripture. Call us or visit our website.

6 Mission Around the World—and at Home

CI's dedication to the mission and message of Jesus goes beyond mere publishing and teacher-training. We make our materials available in the U.S. and all around the world in *prisons, hospitals, orphanages, street ministries*—anywhere the need is great but resources are scarce. CI is a *non-profit ministry* that relies on our modest sales and the benevolence of supporters in our efforts to heed the Great Commission to "go and make disciples of all nations."

Contact Crossways International at 1-800-257-7308 or visit our website at <u>www.crossways.org</u>.

The Structure of the *Crossways* Series

Crossways is offered in six sections of ten units each. Although each section is available for separate purchase, would-be students of the Bible are encouraged to work through all six sections in sequence to gain an overview of the Bible's "big picture." If they choose not to do that, they should first work through a course that will give them an overview of the biblical story-line, such as Crossways International's *See Through the Scriptures* or *The Divine Drama—The Biblical Narrative*. The six sections of *Crossways* are:

From Creation to the Transjordan

Creation; the biblical overture; the patriarchal narratives; the Exodus from Egypt; the Sinai covenant and the Pentateuchal law-codes; the wilderness wanderings.

From the Conquest to the Babylonian Exile

The narratives in Joshua, Judges, 1 and 2 Samuel, 1 and 2 Kings; Worship and Holy War.

The Preexilic and Exilic Prophets

Introducing the Prophets; Amos; Hosea; Isaiah 1–39; Micah; Jeremiah; Nahum, Habakkuk, Zephaniah; Ezekiel.

The Postexilic Period and Judaism

The return from Babylon; the history of the intertestamental period; 1 and 2 Chronicles, Ezra, and Nehemiah; the postexilic prophets; Psalms; Wisdom literature; apocalyptic writings and Daniel, the Apocrypha and Pseudepigrapha; messianic expectations.

The Gospels and Acts

First century Judaism; Mark; Matthew; Luke; John; Acts.

The Letters and Revelation

Paul and his letters; the Catholic letters; Revelation

CROSS WAYS

4 SECTION

UNITS 31–40

The Postexilic Period and Judaism

UNIT 31
Comfort for Captives

Isaiah's Message of Hope to Judah in Exile

Unit 24 dealt with Isaiah 1–39. Unit 31 deals with Isaiah 40–66. Behind the message of the collection of writings referred to as "Isaiah" stand three periods of Israel's history.

1 *Isaiah 1–39* addresses attempts made during the reigns of Ahaz and Hezekiah (735–687 B.C.) to preserve the Davidic dynasty and Jerusalem. It speaks to a situation in which, although the Assyrians hover like a menacing cloud on the horizon, Jerusalem and the Temple are still standing. The general tone of these chapters is one of rebuke and warning. There are hints of difficult times just around the corner, 6:9–13.

2 The historical background to *Isaiah 40–55* is different. These chapters make only one reference to the Davidic dynasty (55:3), and only one reference to the Temple, 44:28 (a debated passage). Judah has been ravaged, the Temple destroyed, and Jerusalem and the cities of Judah have been de-populated, 44:26. The people are in exile, 49:19. The monarchy is no more, 43:28. The Babylonians have replaced the Assyrians as masters of the world, ch. 47. Even so, Babylon's end is near, ch. 47; 48:14,20. Cyrus of Persia is on the march, and is called both the Lord's "shepherd" (meaning, "king") and the Lord's "annointed" (*messiah*), 44:28; 45:1. Cyrus, the Lord's instrument, will make possible the return of the exiles and the rebuilding of Jerusalem and its Temple.

The tone of Isaiah 40–55 is basically one of comfort and hope. Judgment and punishment are things of the past. The discipline of the exile is almost over. Israel's sin has been forgiven. Indeed, the nation has received "double" for all its sins, 40:1,2. The prophet is commissioned to speak "tenderly" to Israel ("Jerusalem"). He is to tell the people that the Lord is coming to release them from captivity, and to take them back to their homeland. The emphasis is on pardon, forgiveness, mercy, restoration, comfort, and hope. The day of rescue is at hand!

3 *Isaiah 56–66* focuses on Jerusalem and implies that the Temple has been rebuilt. It ignores the Davidic dynasty and makes little reference to local or international politics. It attacks abuses in Temple rituals and looks forward to a new *messianic* Jerusalem, 62:1–5; 65:17–66:24. It seems to speak to the postexilic community at a time when its hopes are at a low ebb (538–500 B.C.).

4 The Gentile nations are increasingly included in God's saving plans from Isaiah 1–39 to Isaiah 40–55 to Isaiah 56–66. In the third section, God's goal is to gather all nations into the divine family. The foreign nations are not called to serve as God's instruments to punish a rebellious Israel, but are invited to participate in Israel's salvation. However, those Gentiles who wish to participate must convert to Judaism and observe the Torah.

5 Twenty-first century readers do well to remember that ancient writers knew nothing about modern ideas concerning copyright, acknowledging sources, and so forth. It is likely that much of what has come to us as the writings of an ancient prophet was written by the prophet's scribe (e.g., Jeremiah and Baruch), or the prophet's disciples or "sons," 1 Kings 20:35; 2 Kings 2:3; Amos 7:14. The spirit of a prophet was thought to live on through the ministry of his disciples. They perpetuated his work and directed oracles, written in the *spirit* of their master, to later situations.

6 Considerable debate has taken place concerning the authorship and dating of Isaiah. Some insist that Isaiah of Jerusalem wrote all 66 chapters of the book that bears his name, and view chs. 40–66 as predicting events beyond the prophet's own day. Others believe that chs. 34, 35 and 40–66 date to the sixth century B.C., the period of the Babylonian exile and after. It would seem that although Isaiah 6 describes the prophet's original call and summons to persist, what appear to be new calls to prophesy are recorded in 40:1–11 and 61:1–3.

7 Some scholars note differences between chs. 40–55 and 56–66. Chapters 40–55 are addressed to the exiles still living in Babylon. Chapters 56–66 point to divisions within the postexilic community living in a Judah where the Temple has been rebuilt but the walls of Jerusalem have not been restored, 60:10. It is possible, however, that chs. 34, 35 and 40–66 were written by a single writer during the final years of the Babylonian exile and the first few decades after the return to Judah and Jerusalem.

1 False prophets such as Hananiah predicted that those taken to Babylon in 597 B.C. would return within two years, Jeremiah 28:1–4. Jeremiah rebuked Hananiah and instructed the exiles to prepare for a long stay. Time proved that Jeremiah—and not Hananiah—had spoken "the word of the Lord." However, those enduring the darkness of the exile eventually saw the first rays of the dawn of a new beginning for the people of God. And God used surrounding nations to bring about that new beginning.

2 Nebuchadnezzar ruled from 605 B.C. until 562 B.C. The Babylonian Empire lasted only a little longer than Nebuchadnezzar himself. After his death, political intrigue and murder were rampant. During the period 562–555 B.C., the throne changed hands three times. There was reason for this turmoil: The Babylonian priests coveted greater influence in the realm. Although Nebuchadnezzar had managed to keep them tightly under control, after his death they felt free to pursue their goals—causing considerable instability.

3 After seven years of turmoil, Nabonidus, who was not a direct descendant of Nebuchadnezzar, came to the throne. Nabonidus was a religious fanatic who estranged himself from the priests of Marduk in Babylon and worshipped the moon god Sin. To complicate matters, he set up a royal residence at Tema, a major junction of the caravan routes of Arabia to the southeast of Palestine. He spent many years there, leaving his son Belshazzar to rule Babylon as regent. Because Nabonidus did not worship Marduk, the supreme god of Babylon, and was absent from the city's New Year Festival for ten years, the Babylonian priests detested him. A scroll found in Qumran shows that the dream of Nebuchadnezzar (Daniel 4) was a story told originally of Nabonidus.

4 All was not quiet on the political front. Cyrus of Persia overwhelmed his Median overlord, Astyages, in 550 B.C., and then defeated Croesus of Lydia. Before long, Cyrus' territory stretched from the Persian Gulf to the Aegean Sea. Nabonidus, alarmed by these events, hurried back to Babylon—but it was too late. In 539 B.C. the Persians and Babylonians fought a decisive battle at Opis on the Tigris River. The Persians emerged the victors. A few weeks later, Babylon capitulated to the Persian forces without a struggle, for Babylon's priests literally handed the city over to Cyrus!

5 Cyrus showed himself to be a humane and enlightened ruler. He did not kill Astyages or Croesus, but permitted each to retain a royal retinue. He protected the treasures of the city of Babylon, respected traditional forms of religion, and discontinued the Assyrian and Babylonian practice of deporting captives from conquered territories and breaking down national identities through intermarriage. He permitted conquered peoples to return to their homelands, to restore sacred images to their rightful places, and to rebuild sanctuaries that had been destroyed. In doing so, Cyrus won the affection and respect of conquered peoples. At the same time, Cyrus would not permit restored nations to do anything that would interfere with the political authority of the empire over which he ruled.

6 Although the Judean exiles enjoyed good living conditions in Babylon, they longed to return to their own land. They remained convinced that their history had not come to an end, for God had made remarkable promises to both Abraham and David. Events in Babylon itself gave reason for hope. Jehoiachin, taken to Babylon in 597 B.C., was freed from confinement in 560 B.C., given a position of prestige in the Babylonian court, and apparently lived for a few more years, 2 Kings 25:27–30. Cyrus' rise to power and a growing awareness of his enlightened policies fanned the fires of Jewish nationalism and increased the hope of an eventual return to Judah. Cyrus did not disappoint the exiles. After gaining control of Babylon in 539 B.C., he allowed the exiles to begin returning to Judah in 538 B.C. However, Jehoiachin did not return; he died some years before the first exiles began the long walk back to their homeland.

Numerous themes weave their way through Isaiah 40–55. These appear, disappear, and then reappear as the book unfolds. In the comments that explain **ILLUSTRATION 31C** and **ILLUSTRATION 31D**, these themes are presented in the form of a dialogue between God and the exiles.

Exiles: God, we believed that we, the descendants of Abraham, were your special people. We believed that we would live in the Promised Land forever. But here we are in exile in Babylon. Has our history come to an end?

God: ❶ (*Ishtar Gate in Babylon; road leading to/from it*, top left): I am indeed your God and you are My people. Your time of service in Babylon is over. I am about to rescue you from Babylon and lead you through the wilderness to Jerusalem on a highway. To make this highway, I will cut down the mountains and tip them into the valleys to fill them in. I will make rough places into a plain, and the crooked straight. Your journey home will be quick and comfortable, 40:3–5.

Exiles: Lord, there are many temples in Babylon, and many gods in each one. The priests dress and feed them, wake them each morning, and put them to bed at night. Each year they take them in procession through the city. What will the Babylonian gods think about your plans for us?

God: ❷ (*Babylonian "gods" on the backs of animals*, top right): I, the God of Israel, am the only God. (See 40:25; 42:8; 45:18; 48:12.) The Babylonian gods will think and do nothing because they are nothing (*tree/carved god crossed out*, center right). Their worshippers make them out of wood, cover them with gold, and then carry them around on the backs of animals. However, I made you, and I will carry you. (See 40:18–20; 41:6,7; 42:17; 44:9–20; 45:20; 46:1–7.)

Exiles: But can you really do this?

God: ❸ (*Planet Earth*, center): Certainly! I created the universe and the world. If I can do that, I can rescue you from Babylon.

❹ (*Row of stars stretching from Babylonian ziggurat to Judah*, bottom segment): I can span the heavens with My extended hand, 40:12. Look up at the stars above Babylon! I made them, even as I made those above Jerusalem, 40:25,26. I have given each star a number and a name, call them out each night, and know when even one is missing.

❺ (*Drop of water on hand*, bottom segment): I can hold the waters of the world in the palm of My hand and…

❻ (*Scales and mountains*, bottom segment): …weigh the mountains of the earth in My scales, 40:12.

❼ (*Musical instruments*, bottom segment): You will be so happy to return that you will sing all the way back to Zion, 51:11.

Exiles: We thought that our history was at an end, but now it appears that you have a plan for us.

God: ❽ (*Lighted candle*, center, **and concentric circles radiating out from Judah**, bottom): Indeed! I formed you to be a light to the nations, and to proclaim My salvation to the ends of the earth, 49:6,7.

CREATION 1

EXODUS 1

CREATION 2

EXODUS 2

Exiles: Lord, it is a massive undertaking to rescue us from Babylon and get us back to our land!

God: **1** (**ILLUSTRATION 31D**, *opened waters near Egypt*, *upper segment*): Indeed it is, but don't you remember how I rescued you from Egypt? If I rescued you then, I can do it again.

2 (*Opened waters near Babylon*, *lower segment*): As I opened up the waters to get you out of Egypt, I will open up the waters to get you out of Babylon. (See 43:14–21; 51:9–11.)

Exiles: Lord, it is a long walk back to Judah. How will we know the way? Will we be safe?

God: **3** (*Crown, pillars of fire and cloud*, *lower segment*): I, your King, will go before you to guide you, and behind you to protect you—even as I did when I led you out of Egypt and through the wilderness into the Promised Land, 52:12. And I will be very patient with pregnant mothers, and carry the little children in My arms, 40:11.

Exiles: But when we travelled through the wilderness after leaving Egypt, and when we walked to Babylon, it was so hot. Lack of water was often a problem. Do we have to go through all that again?

God: **4** (*Stream and trees*, *lower segment*): I will provide you with an abundance of water along the way, and see to it that there are plenty of trees for shade. (See 41:17–20; 43:1,2, 14–21; 48:20–22; 49:8–13.) Your journey will be a pleasant and joyous one. Remember what I already told you—you will sing songs all the way back to Judah and Jerusalem (*figures with raised hands*). Don't worry about other nations through whose territory you might pass—they will do all they can to help you get back, 49:22,23. I will deal severely with any who seek to make life difficult for you, 49:24–26.

Exiles: Lord, the Babylonians wrecked our land. Is it even worth returning there?

God: **5** (*Circle around Judah and Jerusalem*, *lower segment*): Yes! I will make it into a new Eden, a new Paradise, a new creation, 51:3. If I could create the universe, I can certainly take care of Judah and Jerusalem, 44:23–28. You will be amazed how rapidly Jerusalem will be rebuilt, 49:17.

Exiles: Lord, we have just a few more questions. You are the only God. You created and control the universe. Why did you allow us to go to Babylon? Have you increased in power lately?

God: **6** I, the eternal One, am not weak. I made a covenant with you—which I honored but you did not. You are in Babylon because I brought you here, because you ignored My covenant with you! (See 42:24,25; 43:22–28; 48:1–11; 51:17–20; 54:7.)

Exiles: How will you get us out from under the Babylonian yoke?

God: **7** My people, I not only made and control the universe, but I direct history as well, 40:21–23. I shall use Cyrus the Persian and his armies to free you from Babylon. Cyrus thinks *he* directs his military campaigns. However, *I* direct him and them to accomplish My will. Cyrus is My shepherd, My anointed one, My messiah. (See 41:2–4, 25–29; 44:28–45:7; 46:8–11.)

Exiles: So you have not forgotten us after all?

God: **8** I will never forget you (40:27-31), and I will never cease to care for you (46:3,4). I can forget you as little as a mother can forget the child at her breast. Your name is tattooed on the palms of My hands, 49:14–16.

Exiles: We are so few. Can we become a great people again?

God: Remember your origins! I began your history with only two people—Abraham and Sarah. I formed a large nation from them, 51:1,2. Before you know where you are, your numbers will be so great there will hardly be enough room for you in Judah, 49:19–21.

Exiles: Lord, what moves You to be so good to us?

God: I do not act because of what is in *you*, but because of what is in *Me*. I act for My name's sake. My reasons flow from kindness, grace, and love! (See 43:25; 44:21,22; 48:9–11.)

Exiles: You still have a purpose for us, then?

God: Most certainly! I formed you to be My witnesses (43:10), My light to the nations (42:6; 49:6), a people to glorify Me (49:3), My servant people (41:8,9; 42:1–4; 44:1; 49:3). All that you have gone through in Babylon is no accident. It has been My way of disciplining you for ignoring My covenant. I am using the experience to mold you into the servant people I always intended you to be.

A key thought runs through all the above dialogue. The prophet is to speak tenderly to the exiles and assure them that they are about to be released, not simply from the bonds of *captivity*, but also from the bonds of *guilt*. The Lord has forgiven Israel, not because Israel's suffering has wiped out some debt of punishment that had to be paid, but because God acts in mercy and love to create new life and new beginnings for His people. God acts in mercy and love because of what is in His heart—not because of the people's practice of any sacrificial system.

A profound issue emerges in Isaiah 40–66. A brief summary of the issue follows.

1 It is traditional to speak of four "Servants Songs" in Isaiah 40–66, namely:
- 42:1–4: The servant—a light to the nations.
- 49:1–6: The servant's mission.
- 50:4–11: The servant's humiliation and vindication.
- 52:13–53:12: The suffering servant.

2 In a *positive* way, the servant is God's beloved one, either all Israel (41:8–9; 43:10; 44:1–5), or the prophet and his disciples (42:1; 49:3,6) on whom the Israelites or the nations fix their attention, 50:10; 52:13; 53:11. Even Cyrus the Persian is included among God's servants, 44:28.

3 In a *negative* way, the servant is *Israel*—blind, deaf, robbed of dignity (42:19), guilty, and sinful, 43:23. Israel's sins and iniquities have caused God deep pain, and burdened and wearied Him, 43:24.

4 In Isaiah 56–66, only the plural form "servants" is used. It is used to refer to faithful Israelites (63:17) or to foreigners called to serve at the Temple, 56:6.

5 The servant's role is as follows: God elects the servant and commissions him to proclaim His message of truth and righteousness to the world. God will empower the servant with the divine spirit to overcome obstacles that he will encounter. Although the servant will at first meet with failure, God will empower the servant to become the savior of his fellow Jews—and finally of the whole earth. The final servant song (52:13–53:12) describes the servant as a martyr and outcast who lays down his life for others.

6 Much debate has taken place with regard to the identity of the servant.
- Was it Israel, 49:3?
- Was it a small group within Israel?
- Was it an individual?
- Was it an historical figure or someone to come?
- Was it the prophet himself?

7 The servant theme, with its message of warning and comfort, influenced the early postexilic community. After all, the servant's mission was to make God known to all the nations so that the whole world might share in God's salvation.

8 The early disciples eventually saw the roles of suffering servant and royal messiah combined in Jesus, Matthew 20:24–28; Mark 10:41–45; Luke 9:21. Without doubt, Isaiah's servant songs profoundly influenced the formulation of Christian belief and mission.

1 The writer expresses the hope that the Gentiles will embrace God's plan of salvation, and looks forward to the day when God will create new heavens and a new earth, 56:1–8; 65:17–66:24.

2 In chs. 56–59, the writer shows concern for Temple worship, Sabbath observance, and the practice of justice and compassion in everyday life. In 56:1–8 he permits even outcasts (such as eunuchs) to enter the Temple. Foreigners living outside the Promised Land (who had converted to Judaism) were also granted the right of entry into the Temple. It is important to note how Matthew 21:13, Luke 19:46, and Mark 11:17 handle this hope. Only Mark speaks of Jesus attacking the Jerusalem authorities for excluding the Gentiles from the Temple.

3 Chs. 63–66 deal with matters referred to in chs. 56–59 (point 2 above), but in reverse order. Isaiah 63:1–6 contains an attack on the Edomites who helped the Babylonians destroy Judah and Jerusalem in 587 B.C.

4 In 64:1, the prophet begs God to rend the heavens asunder and to come down to earth to reveal the divine presence. This hope came to pass at Jesus' baptism, Mark 1:9–11.

5 Isaiah of Jerusalem (chs. 1–39) echoed the conviction of other prophets that Jerusalem would not fall to the Syria/Israel alliance in 735 B.C. or to the Assyrians in 701 B.C. because of God's covenant with David. However, Isaiah 40–66 stresses the Exodus motif and refers to the Davidic covenant only once—in 55:3–5. Even then, in 55:3–5 the everlasting covenant is made with all Israelites who respond to the Lord's call. The prophet's concern is to speak words of assurance to all who have suffered as a result of the Babylonian exile. He assures them that their sufferings will bring healing and blessings to the nations. Isaiah chs. 56–66 make no reference to David.

THE CONTINUING ROLES OF THE SINAI AND DAVIDIC COVENANTS

1 The prophets based their attacks on Israel on the Sinai Covenant. Because the people broke the covenant, the covenant curses came into effect. Although Isaiah 1–39 also echoed this conviction, Isaiah of Jerusalem insisted that Jerusalem would not fall to the Syria/Israel alliance in 735 B.C. or to the Assyrians in 701 B.C. because of God's covenant with David.

2 Isaiah 40–66 stresses the Exodus motif, but makes little mention of the covenant with David and the election of Jerusalem. Reference is made to the Davidic covenant only once: an invitation is extended to all nations to attend the great banquet of the end time. Even then, the everlasting covenant is made, not with David, but with all Israelites who respond to the Lord's call, Isaiah 55:3–5. The prophet's concern is to speak words of assurance to Israel, whose sufferings will bring healing and blessings to the nations.

Throughout Isaiah 1–39, 40–55, and 56–66 one senses an increasing desire to embrace, and become involved in, God's plan of salvation for Israel. Political developments influenced theological thought.

1 In 1:1,2, the prophet calls on the heavens and the earth.

2 Chapters 2–12 begin and end with a reference to the Temple. Ch. 2:2–4 contains a vision of the nations streaming to the Temple on Mt. Zion. In 12:3–6, the prophet looks forward to the time when those who worship on Mt. Zion will make God's deeds known among the nations.

3 Chapters 24–27 refer to the Lord wiping away tears from all faces (25:8) and bringing outcasts from Assyria and Egypt to "the holy mountain at Jerusalem," 27:13.

4 Chapters 28–35 invite the blind, lame, sick, dumb, and underprivileged to partake of the Lord's salvation, 35:5,6.

5 In 49:6, Israel is referred to as a *light to the nations*.

6 There are suggestions that the day will come when some of the (converted) Gentiles will lead worship rituals shoulder to shoulder with the priests and Levites, 56:6; 66:18–21.

7 Chapter 19:24–25 refers to Egypt and Assyria as being equal with Israel. It reads:

> On that day Israel will be a third with Egypt and Assyria, a blessing in the midst of the earth, whom the lord of hosts has blessed, saying, "Blessed be Egypt My people, and Assyria the work of My hands, and Israel My heritage."

8 Not all later Jewish thinkers and writers could accept this spirit of universalism. When later rabbis translated 19:25 into the daily language of the people (Greek and Aramaic), they edited the meaning:

Greek: *Blessed be My people who are in Egypt and who are in Assyria, and My inheritance Israel.*

Aramaic: *Blessed be My people whom I brought out of Egypt. Because they sinned against Me, I carried them into exile to Assyria, but now that they have repented, they shall be My people and My inheritance Israel.*

31E *Isaiah 1–39* addresses events from about 735–701 B.C., during which period the Assyrians destroyed the Northern Kingdom of Israel and hovered on Judah's horizon in a threatening manner. The writer's central concern is what must be done to preserve the Davidic dynasty, Judah, Jerusalem, and the Temple.

Isaiah 40–55 speaks to the situation that prevailed after 587 B.C. when the Babylonians devastated Judah, Jerusalem, and the Temple, and took thousands of Judeans into exile in Babylon. However, Babylon's days are numbered; Persia will soon gain control Mesopotamia.

Isaiah 56–66 speaks to a people who have returned to Judah but whose hopes are at a low ebb. It makes no reference to the Davidic dynasty but focuses on Jerusalem and the role of its rebuilt Temple.

31B Although the exiles taken to Babylon enjoyed good living conditions there, many longed to return to Judah. In 539 B.C., Cyrus the Persian conquered Babylonia and incorporated it into his empire. In 538 B.C., he permitted the Jewish exiles to return to their own land. Because the two Davidic kings taken to Babylon—Jehoiachin and Zedekiah—died before the return began, the Davidic dynasty was no more.

31C Isaiah 40–55 might be read as a dialog between God and the exiles in Babylon. God assures the exiles that He will come swiftly and powerfully to rescue them and lead them back to Judah and Jerusalem. Nothing can prevent that from happening. The exiles should be filled with joy and confidence. Their God is not one among many, but the *only God*. God holds dominion, not just over that little tract of ground called Judah, but over the whole earth. The "gods" of all Gentile peoples are "nothings." Their gods do not even exist. Artisans carve them out of wood, just as they might make a piece of furniture. These false gods cannot carry anyone anywhere, but must themselves be carried from place to place. However, God can and will carry the exiles back to Judah and Jerusalem.

31D There need be no doubt about whether God can do what He promises. God created and owns the universe—and He rescued His people from slavery in Egypt. If that creator-owner God could carry out the first "exodus," the first rescue of His people, He can do it again—and will! Even more, He will transform creation and restore the splendors of the original Eden. However, although Israel is God's special people, it is not called to idleness. It is called to be a light to the nations and to make the Lord's existence, will, and mercy known to humanity.

31E Israel is called to be the Lord's Servant to the nations—a role that can result in the people suffering the kind of pain they experienced during the destructions of 597 B.C. and 587 B.C., and the exile itself. Israel's present suffering, then, is not merely the result of the nation's disobedience; it is taking place so that Israel and the nations might be healed and brought into true fellowship with God.

31F In chs. 56–66, the hope of a universal restoration of creation and healing of humanity is expressed. The message focuses on Temple worship, Sabbath observance, and the practice of justice and compassion in everyday life. The hope is that nations will embrace the faith of Israel and acknowledge the Lord to be the true and only God. Even so, 63:1–6 expresses hatred of the Edomites who plundered Judah after the Babylonians devastated Judah and Jerusalem in 587 B.C. If only God would tear the heavens apart and reveal His divine presence to His people! (It is significant that these chapters make no reference to the restoration of the Davidic dynasty.)

31G A variety of hopes in relation to God's people and the Gentiles surface in Isaiah. Numerous passages express compassion to those suffering physical disabilities in Israel, hope concerning the return to the Promised Land of the Jews scattered around the Mediterranean world, and the hope that the Gentiles will embrace the Jewish faith and join the Jews in worship. However, later Jewish thinkers and teachers rejected the spirit of universalism expressed in parts of Isaiah.

CROSS WAYS

4 SECTION

UNITS 31–40

The Postexilic Period and Judaism

UNIT 32
1 and 2 Chronicles

The Chronicler's Message to Postexilic Judah

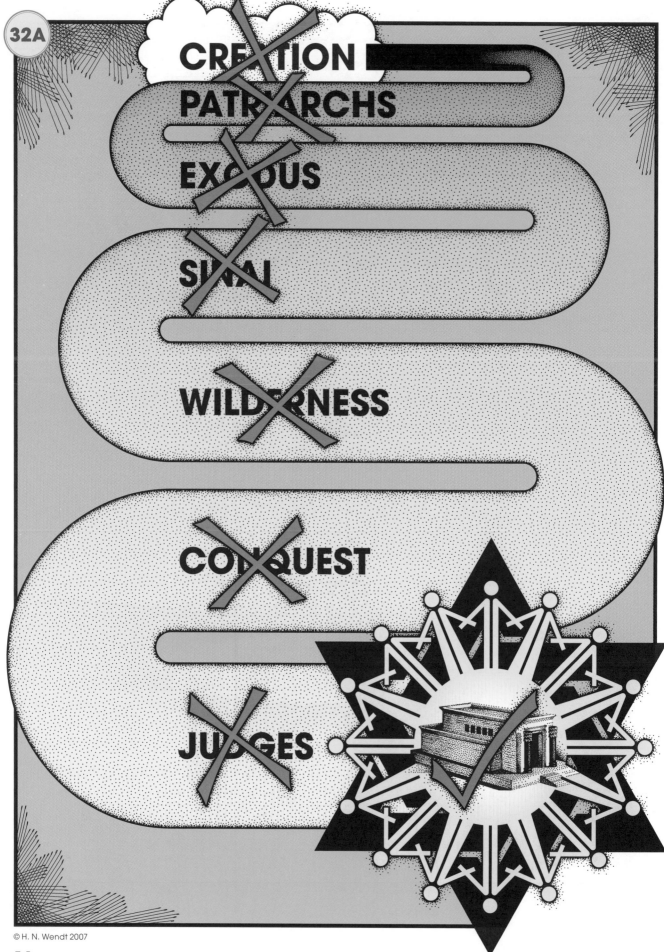

CREATION
PATRIARCHS
EXODUS
SINAI
WILDERNESS
CONQUEST
JUDGES

1 First and Second Chronicles, Ezra, and Nehemiah constitute a collection of writings traditionally referred to as the work of the Chronicler. Because similar theological emphases run through these four books, they are thought to be the product of one writer or a single school. Opinions differ as to when they were written. Various dates within the period 400–200 B.C. are suggested.

2 The Greek title for these books is *paraleipomena*, or "things passed over" (in Samuel and Kings). However, the writings of the Chronicler are more than a supplement to Samuel and Kings. A comparison of the two narratives reveals differences in scope and purpose.

First and Second Chronicles outline the growth of humanity and the Israelites from Adam until 587 B.C. as some within the postexilic community understood that period. In selecting and editing the events he included in his work, the Chronicler sought to give direction to his contemporaries—a direction that would ensure the continuation of a people that had suffered destruction and exile. He emphasizes, therefore:

- The exile was a catastrophe. It must never be permitted to happen again.
- If the Israelites are to fulfill their God-given mission and once again experience the glory that was theirs during the days of David, they must strive to be the kind of people God intended them to be.

The Chronicler's purpose was to reveal the ways and actions of the living God (as he understood them) in the affairs of humanity *at the time he wrote.*

3 Ezra and Nehemiah (Unit 33) summarize the first 150 years of the history of postexilic Judah and list the theological emphases that surfaced during that period:

- Cyrus' edict of liberation;
- The exiles' return to Jerusalem;
- The rebuilding of the Temple;
- The antagonism of the new community's neighbors;
- The rebuilding of Jerusalem's walls;
- The renewal of the covenant in the life of the nation.

4 In the first nine chapters of 1 Chronicles, the writer uses genealogical tables to cover the period from the beginning of time (signified by the ***cloud***, *top* of **ILLUSTRATION 32A**) to Saul, 9:35–44. The only information the writer gives about events in Saul's life (a *Benjaminite*) is, ironically, an account of his death, 1 Chronicles 10. However, the writer shows great interest in the tribe of *Judah*, 1 Chronicles 2:3–17.

5 The first nine chapters in 1 Chronicles make no reference to:

- ***CREATION***
- The period of the ***PATRIARCHS***
- The ***EXODUS*** from Egypt
- The events at ***SINAI***
- The ***WILDERNESS*** period
- The ***CONQUEST*** under Joshua
- The period of the ***JUDGES***

Hence, in **ILLUSTRATION 32A** these events are listed and crossed out.

6 ***Star of David, community around the Jerusalem Temple, approval symbol:*** The Chronicler then devotes nineteen chapters to the life of David, 1 Chronicles 11–29. His goals are:

- To establish and defend the legitimate claims of the Davidic dynasty in Israel's history;
- To underscore the place of Jerusalem and its divinely established Temple worship as the center of religious life for the Jewish community of his day.

The narrative implies that if Judaism is to survive and prosper, it must heed the lessons of the past and serve God in the place where He has chosen to dwell—the Jerusalem Temple. From the Chronicler's point of view, David's reign is the ideal to which all subsequent rule in Judah must aspire.

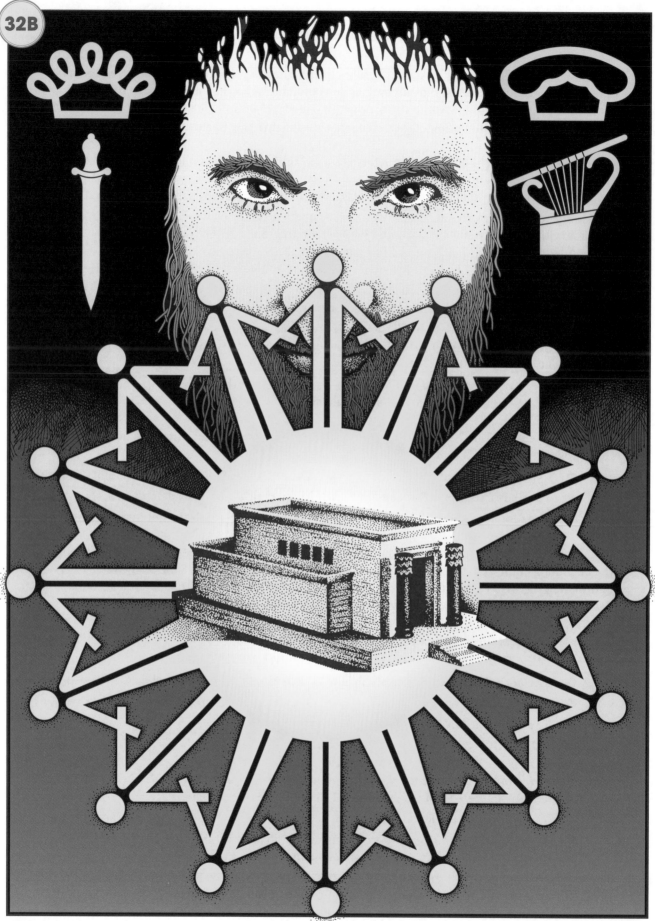

The Chronicler's David

1 The Chronicler devotes one chapter to Saul's life, introducing him only to dispose of him, 1 Chronicles 10. Although the Chronicler's description of Saul's suicide resembles that in 1 Samuel 31:1–13, it omits reference to the indecent exposure of the bodies of Saul and his sons, and emphasizes the reasons for Saul's tragic end, 1 Chronicles 10:13,14. All of Saul's sons are wiped out at the battle of Gilboa; compare this with 1 Samuel 31 (where only three of Saul's sons are killed). Saul is seen merely as an obstacle to the breaking in of David's kingship—as one who needs to be removed from the stage of history as quickly as possible.

2 The *face* depicted in **ILLUSTRATION 32B** is that of *David*. The Chronicler's version of David is very different from that contained in 1 Samuel 16:1 through 1 Kings 2:9. It contains no reference to any of David's sins. Rather, it focuses on how David (***crown and sword***, *top left*):

● Established Israel as a nation;

● Captured Jerusalem and made it the nation's key religious center;

● Made preparations for the construction of the ***Temple*** *that Solomon eventually built.*

The writer's central conviction is that the history of Israel (and the world!) took place so that the *Jerusalem Temple* might eventually be built and the ***community of Israel*** might worship the God of Israel within its walls. David himself is considered an almost ecclesiastical monarch (***priest's hat and psalmist's harp***, *top right*). The Chronicler gives the impression that Israel's true beginning should not be linked to the events of the Exodus and Sinai, but to the rise of David.

3 David is the apple of the Chronicler's eye. He outlines the life of David in four segments:

 a. David is made king of Judah and Israel, chs. 11,12; note also ch. 17 and 2 Samuel 7.

 b. David brings the Ark of the Covenant to Jerusalem, chs. 13–16.

 c. David expands his realm, chs. 18–20.

 d. David prepares for the building of the Temple, chs. 21–29.

4 In Samuel and Kings, David is presented as a *political* leader, a man with strengths and weaknesses that endeared him to his people as the greatest king ever. The Chronicler, however, shows only a limited interest in David's political genius. This is understandable, for by the time he wrote, Israel had ceased to be a nation. To be sure, the Chronicler did revel in David's military accomplishments and the splendor of his realm (1 Chronicles 18–20), and emphasized also the Nathan oracle—based on a covenant of Divine Commitment, 1 Chronicles 17; see also 2 Samuel 7. However, for the Chronicler, *David was primarily the one who organized Israel as a worshiping community.* It was David who:

● Made Jerusalem, the Holy City, his religious capital.

● Planned the building of the Temple according to God's directions, 1 Chronicles 28:19.

● Organized the music of the Temple and assigned the Levites their duties.

Although 2 Samuel 6 says that *David alone* made the decision to bring the Ark of the Covenant to Jerusalem, the Chronicler says the move was sanctioned by *all the people*, 1 Chronicles 13:1–5.

5 The ecclesiastical robes in which the writer dresses David, the religious founding father, tend to cover David the man. Therefore, among the things that the Chronicler does not mention are the following:

 a. David's troubles with, and flights from, Saul, 1 Samuel 18–26.

 b. David's early "on the run" career in the wilderness.

 c. David's slaughter of the Amalekites, 1 Samuel 27:8–12.

d. David's attempt to obtain the favor of Judah's elders, 1 Samuel 30:26–30.

e. The early wars between Judah and Israel, 2 Samuel 2:12–17; 3:1.

f. Ishbosheth's period of rule in Israel, 2 Samuel 2:8–10.

g. Joab's murder of Abner, 2 Samuel 3:22–30.

h. David's slaughter of Jerusalem's lame and blind, 2 Samuel 5:8.

i. David's harem, 2 Samuel 3:2–5; 5:13–16; 15:16; 16:15–22.

j. David's adultery with Bathsheba and murder of Uriah, 2 Samuel 11,12.

k. Amnon's rape of Tamar, 2 Samuel 13:1–19.

l. Absalom's murder of Amnon, flight, return, revolt, and death, 2 Samuel 13:20–18:33.

m. Sheba's revolt, 2 Samuel 20.

n. The execution of Saul's sons and grandsons, 2 Samuel 21.

o. The struggle between Adonijah and Solomon for the throne, 1 Kings 1.

p. David's deathbed instructions to Solomon to kill Joab and Shimei, 1 Kings 2:1–9.

6. The Chronicler declares that to the very last, David's mind was engrossed with dreams about the future Temple, 1 Chronicles 28,29. The last words the Chronicler attributes to David constitute one of the finest prayers in the Old Testament, 1 Chronicles 29:10–19.

7. According to 2 Samuel 24:24, David bought the real estate on which the Temple would eventually be built for 50 shekels of silver (about twenty American dollars). However, according to 1 Chronicles 21:25, he paid 600 shekels of gold for it (about 10,000 American dollars). Similarly, the Chronicler speaks of 3,775 tons of gold and 37,750 tons of silver being used in the construction of the Temple, 1 Chronicles 22:14. (Whether or not these numbers are to be taken literally is debatable.) From his personal fortune, David gave the equivalent of 115 tons of gold and 265 tons of silver for use in the construction of the Temple, 1 Chronicles 29:3,4. The Temple and the ground on which it stands were very precious, indeed!

The Chronicler's Solomon

1. The Chronicler outlines the reign of Solomon with a similar emphasis. So keen is the Chronicler to praise Solomon's reign that he suggests it was even more glorious than that of David, 1 Chronicles 29:25; but see 2 Kings 18:5, 23:25.

2. The Chronicler does not mention:
   a. Solomon's struggle for the throne, 1 Chronicles 23:1ff; 28:3ff; 29:1,22b.
   b. Solomon's use of *Israelite* slave labor, 2 Chronicles 2:17,18; 8:7–10.
   c. Solomon's gift of twenty Galilean cities to *Hiram* of Tyre, 1 Kings 9:10–14. According to 2 Chronicles 8:1,2, *Huram* of Tyre gave cities to Solomon. The transaction is reversed!
   d. The many wives of both Solomon and his son Rehoboam, 2 Chronicles 11:21.
   e. Solomon's idolatry, 1 Kings 11:1–13; 2 Kings 23:13,14.

3. Solomon does not permit one of his wives (pharaoh's daughter) to live in Jerusalem, 2 Chronicles 8:11.

4. In relation to the Temple:
   a. Second Chronicles 3:1 links the Temple site to Mt. Moriah, where Genesis 22:2 says Abraham made preparations to sacrifice his son, Isaac.
   b. The Chronicler suggests that the front porch of the Temple was 180 feet (55 meters) high—triple the height of the free-standing columns near the Temple's entrance, 2 Chronicles 3:3,4,15.
   c. While 1 Kings 6:31 says the Holy of Holies was separated from the Holy Place by doors made of *olive wood*, the Chronicler says the two areas were separated by a *curtain*, 2 Chronicles 3:14. The Chronicler also provides Solomon with a platform on which to pray (2 Chronicles 6:13); in the postexilic period only the priests were permitted to pray before the altar.

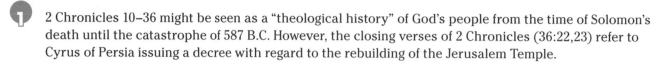

Kings of ISRAEL

1 2 Chronicles 10–36 might be seen as a "theological history" of God's people from the time of Solomon's death until the catastrophe of 587 B.C. However, the closing verses of 2 Chronicles (36:22,23) refer to Cyrus of Persia issuing a decree with regard to the rebuilding of the Jerusalem Temple.

2 The writer pays only passing attention to the Northern Kingdom and mentions its history only when he must do so to make sense out of the history of Judah. His conviction is that the Northern Kingdom never really belonged to the people of God. Why not? It had cut itself off from the Davidic dynasty (the only *legitimate dynasty*) and did not encourage worship in the Temple (the only *legitimate shrine*) at Jerusalem (the only place in which God made His name to dwell), 2 Chronicles 6:5,6 and 13:1–12, especially vv. 5,8. The Chronicler does not mention the Assyrian destruction of the Northern Kingdom in 721 B.C.

Later Kings of JUDAH

1 Although the Chronicler idealizes the reigns of David and Solomon, what he has to say about later kings is based on the concept of retribution for neglect of God's will. He relates the fate of each king to his religious, or irreligious, conduct.

2 The following reward/punishment associations occur in 2 Chronicles:

    a. Shishak's invasion of Judah is related to Rehoboam's disobedience, 12:2–12.

    b. Asa is afflicted with diseased feet soon after behaving unwisely, 16:7–12.

    c. Jehoshaphat's maritime ventures fail because they involve fellowship with Ahaziah, a northern king, 20:35–37.

    d. Uzziah is afflicted with leprosy because of his pride, 26:16–23.

    e. It seems inconceivable that God should have permitted a king as wicked as Manasseh to reign for so long; hence, in Chronicles he repents, 33:10–13; see 2 Kings 21:10–16.

    f. Josiah's death at the hands of Pharaoh Neco is not without cause, 35:20–25; see 2 Kings 23:28–30.

3 The point is: *Do not treat God lightly! God takes a dim view of disobedience. God treats the nation as He treats its kings. Therefore, be the kind of kings and the kind of people you were intended to be.*

1 The work of the Chronicler constitutes a "theological history" of Israel's worship life centering in Zion. Accordingly, despite the account of David's life in 2 Samuel 16–1 Kings 2:12, the Chronicler says David made preparations for the building of the Temple, planned its worship life, and organized the priestly groups who would function within its walls. He thus looks beyond David to the Temple—and beyond the Temple to God.

Why does he do this? The way to avoid a repetition of the exile is to take the God worshiped in the Jerusalem Temple as seriously as possible. If David took such interest in the Temple, postexilic Israel should follow his example.

2 What does this imply for Israel's spiritual life? To begin with, it is essential that Israel be obedient to God. The Chronicler stresses this through the manner in which he outlines the period from Solomon until 587 B.C. To illustrate, 2 Chronicles contains 822 verses, of which 480 describe the reigns of four pious kings and 342 summarize the reigns of seventeen other kings. In doing this, the Chronicler frequently uses words such as *law*, *commandment*, *statutes*, and related terms that have to do with reward and punishment.

3 Furthermore, Israel is called to be a *worshiping community*, a kingdom of priests and a holy nation, Exodus 19:5,6. It is called to be a people whose life is a liturgy and a divine service. Its activities are to center around the Jerusalem Temple where priests and Levites are to play an indispensable role in the conduct of worship rituals. Even a cursory reading of the Chronicler's record shows his interest in liturgical activities. Festival and worship services are frequently described, and the people are always ready to participate in them. For example, the people experience such joy in observing Hezekiah's Passover that they decide to observe it a second time the following week, 2 Chronicles 30:23.

4 The Chronicler shows a special interest in those people set aside to supervise the worship life of the nation, namely the priests and Levites, and frequently stresses the importance of their role in the nation's worship life. The priests and Levites even take part in military ventures. The writer takes care to distinguish the priests and Levites from the laity, and omits all previous references to laymen participating in a religious function or entering a holy area. Accordingly, David's sons are not priests, but officials, 2 Samuel 8:18; 1 Chronicles 18:17. Only priests can take part in the coup which dethrones Athaliah; after all, the event takes place in the Temple, 2 Kings 11:4–20; 2 Chronicles 23.

1 In the Chronicler's writings, the focal point in Israel's history shifts from the Exodus event to the establishment of the Jerusalem Temple and the inauguration of its worship and rituals—and the pivotal role David and his successors played in establishing the Temple system.

2 The Chronicler manifests an intense dislike for anything related to the Northern Kingdom. It is possible that he adopts this attitude to prove to the northern Samaritans the legitimacy of the Davidic dynasty and the worship life centered in the Jerusalem Temple. The Samaritans had cut themselves off from Judah and its worship life about the time the Chronicler was writing.

3 The anti-Israel (Northern Kingdom) polemic is revealed in numerous ways. When Abijah of Judah joins in battle with Jeroboam I, he delivers a speech prior to the battle. In the speech, Abijah declares it a foregone conclusion that the northern armies will be defeated. Why? The northerners do not submit to the Davidic dynasty and have established an illegitimate priesthood, 2 Chronicles 13:4–12. Hence, the Chronicler refers to many from the north fleeing to the south when they observe that the Lord is with Asa, 2 Chronicles 15:9.

4 The Chronicler shows a greater interest in the tribe of Benjamin than any other except Judah and Levi. In the postexilic period, much of the former territory of Benjamin became attached to Judah, 1 Chronicles 8:1–40; 9:7–9; Nehemiah 11:7–9.

5 Significant comments are made about the Ark of the Covenant and the Tabernacle. However, they are at different locations. The Ark is in *Jerusalem* and the Tabernacle is at *Gibeon*, 1 Chronicles 16:1,37–42; 21:28–22:1 (see Unit 20). The two come together when Solomon dedicates the Temple, 2 Chronicles 5:2–7.

6 The Chronicler's use of numbers gives rise to debate. His numbers (such as those referred to in 2 Chronicles 3:3,4,15) should not be seen as a statistical problem, but as a preliminary glimpse of the grandeur, splendor, and abundance that will be Israel's when finally the nation enters the Messianic Age—the focus of all its hopes.

7 Although the monarchy was a thing of the past when the Chronicler wrote, his picture of David is designed to encourage the faithful to look for the time when the promise made to David (2 Samuel 7; 1 Chronicles 17) will be realized. When that time comes, David's Messianic descendant will be as little like the previous kings of Judah as possible. Hence, his account of David describes the David that *should have been*, rather than the David that *actually was*. He is giving his readers a glimpse of the ideal Messianic king that many believed would eventually come. These points are admittedly hypothetical. It may be that the Chronicler's account of David is meant to focus attention solely on the Temple and, above all, on the God of that Temple.

1. The central concern of 1 and 2 Chronicles, and Ezra and Nehemiah, is to defend the legitimacy of the Davidic dynasty and the Jerusalem Temple. God can be properly worshiped only at the Jerusalem Temple. The writer outlines how that worship life was:
   a. *Established* by David (1 Chronicles 11–29) and Solomon (2 Chronicles 1–9);
   b. *Lost through the disobedience* of the kings of Judah (2 Chronicles 10–36);
   c. *Restored* (Ezra and Nehemiah).

2. A central concern of the Chronicler's account is to show that Israel can secure its future by continuing to worship God according to the pattern set by David. Hence, the Chronicler presents the Judah of his day as a worshipping community that is a direct extension of the worshipping community God established centuries before through David. Its social and religious structures are those that David created at God's command.

3. Israel's hopes, then, did not reside in what a messiah might be able to accomplish or reveal sometime in the future. Israel could secure its future by carefully honoring the religious institutions and practices revealed by God to David, handed down to Judah's priests, and kept alive by the remnant that survived the exile and returned to Jerusalem.

4. The Chronicler viewed the exile as merely an unfortunate interruption in the otherwise unbroken history of Judah as a worshipping community. In the Chronicler's scheme of things, the reestablishment of the monarchy was not as important as the reestablishment of the proper worship of God in Jerusalem. The people who supported and worshipped at the Temple fulfilled all the important tasks of the period of the monarchy.

5. When the Chronicler wrote, not all of Abraham's descendants recognized the Jerusalem Temple as the only legitimate place of worship. There was a temple dedicated to the worship of God on Mt. Gerizim in Samaria. The destruction of the Samaritan temple in 128 B.C. by the Jewish Hasmonean king, John Hyrcanus, led to the final break between Jews and Samaritans. Another temple was erected on Elephantine Island (near present-day Aswan in Egypt) to serve a Jewish military colony located there. The Chronicler does not mention the worship sites Jeroboam established at Bethel and Dan. For him, there could be only one Temple—that in Jerusalem. In his estimation, the northerners did not have a true priesthood; their worship was invalid and useless, 2 Chronicles 13:9.

6. Did the Chronicler achieve his goal? Hardly! Later units will point out that, as time went by, the Essenes opposed the Hasmoneans, the Pharisees had disputes with the Sadducees, and the Herodians fought with the Zealots. Although the Pharisees survived the fall of Jerusalem in A.D. 70 and gave rise to rabbinic Judaism, groups in Babylon (*Kairites*) refused to accept the authority of the rabbis. Still today, some *Orthodox* rabbis do not accept the legitimacy of *Conservative* and *Reformed* varieties of Judaism.

32A First and Second Chronicles, Ezra, and Nehemiah are referred to as the work of the Chronicler. They were written between 400–200 B.C. The Chronicler demonstrates little interest in Israel's history prior to David. He makes no mention of the patriarchal period, the Exodus and Sinai events, the conquest under Joshua, the period of the judges, and Saul's reign prior to his death. He concentrates on the reigns of David and Solomon, emphasizing the role each played in planning and building the Jerusalem Temple. A cause-and-effect principle is applied to the histories of the kings who follow Solomon.

32B The Chronicler devotes only one chapter to the life and reign of Saul—introducing him so that he and his sons might be removed from the scene as quickly as possible. The Chronicler's version of David's life is very different from that outlined in 1 Samuel 16:1–Kings 2:9. Any detail that might show David (and also Solomon) in a bad light is omitted. The writer focuses on how David established Israel as a nation, captured Jerusalem and made it the nation's key religious center, made preparations for the construction of the Temple that Solomon built, and planned the worship practices that would eventually be carried out within its walls.

32C Because Solomon built the Temple that his father designed, his reign is seen to be more glorious than that of David. Any negative aspect of Solomon's reign (referred to in 1 Kings 1–11) is omitted. Not only did David pay a huge sum of money for the land on which the Temple was built, but Solomon used vast quantities of gold and silver to adorn the Temple itself.

32D The Chronicler's narrative might be understood as a theological history rather than a factual narrative. The writer makes only limited reference to the history of the Northern Kingdom; it had cut itself off from the Davidic dynasty, and did not permit it citizens to worship in the Jerusalem Temple.

32E When reporting the history of Judah beyond the time of Solomon, the Chronicler links the worth and fate of each king to his religious or irreligious conduct. The yardstick used in evaluating the worth of a king is whether or not he promoted the worship of one God in one place (the Jerusalem Temple) as David had done.

32E A central concern of the Chronicler is to avoid a repetition of the Babylonian campaigns of 597 and 587 B.C. that resulted in the destruction of Judah, Jerusalem, and the Temple—and the experience of the Babylonian exile. He emphasizes the importance of worship rituals and the observance of festivals—in which the Temple priests and Levites are to play a central role. No reference is made to laymen playing a role in leading worship activities or entering a holy area.

32F The Chronicler's focus is not on the Exodus from Egypt and the Sinai covenant, but on the importance of the Temple and the worship rituals that take place within its walls. He makes numerous references to the Tabernacle and the Ark of the covenant—which are located in different places. When referring to the number of priests who served at the Temple and the quantities of precious metals used in building the Temple, the concern is not statistical accuracy. It is rather to provide God's people with a preliminary glimpse of the glory of the coming Messianic Age. The people can hasten the coming of the Messianic Age by worshiping at the Jerusalem Temple in the manner outlined in the Chronicler's writings.

32G The Chronicler wrote to assure his readers that Judah's future depended on worshiping God correctly in the Temple that David planned and Solomon built. The focus is not political history, but proper worship practices that some of Solomon's successors tried to maintain.

CROSS WAYS

4 SECTION

UNITS 31–40

The Postexilic Period and Judaism

UNIT 33

A New Beginning

Events in the Early Postexilic Period;
The Message and Work of Haggai and Zechariah, Ezra and Nehemiah

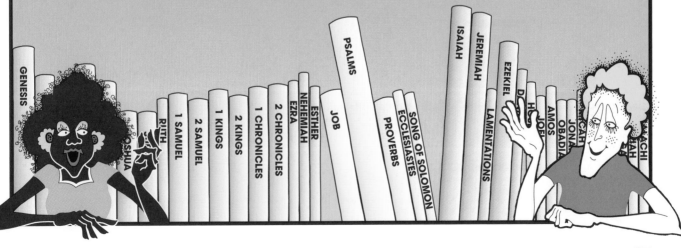

33A

The contents of Ezra and Nehemiah deal with two major issues:

- The rebuilding of the Jerusalem Temple.
- The reordering of Jewish life.

1 *Rubble, lower left:* After Cyrus the Persian gained control of Babylon in 539 B.C., he issued a decree permitting all captive peoples to return to their homelands. Some of the Jewish exiles in Babylon returned to Judea the following year under the leadership of Sheshbazzar. Other groups returned under the leadership of Joshua and Zerubbabel. Although many of the exiles expected to return to a Judah and Jerusalem that were literally a Garden of Eden (Isaiah 51:1–3), they returned to a Judah and Jerusalem that were largely rubble!

2 *Small stone altar amidst rubble, lower left:* The returning exiles built an *altar* among the rubble in Jerusalem and began offering sacrifices, Ezra 3:1–6.

3 *Temple, lower left:* Although work began on rebuilding the Temple (Ezra 3:6–13), the project suffered delays. After all, the new community faced many difficulties, not the least of which was poverty. They also encountered opposition from those who remained living in Judah during the exile, and from the Samaritans to the north. In 520 B.C., the prophets Haggai and Zechariah began exhorting the exiles to finish the building project, with the result that the new structure was dedicated in 515 B.C. Although it is not known precisely what the new structure looked like (**question mark**), there are indications that it was less ornate than Solomon's Temple had been.

4 *Bricks in circle around Judah and Jerusalem:* Eventually—perhaps 75–100 years later—Nehemiah and Ezra returned to make their own contribution to the life of the Judean community. Nehemiah's major contribution was to provide inspiration and leadership for the rebuilding of Jerusalem's walls.

This project met with stern opposition from *Sanballat of Samaria* (**face**, *top left*) and *Tobiah, the Ammonite* (**face**, *top right*). Nehemiah refused to permit these two individuals to take part in any of the restored community's activities. Although Sanballat had a Babylonian name, Sin-ubbalit (*Sin, the Moon God, Has Given Life*), two of his sons had names referring to the God of Israel—suggesting that they may have worshiped the same God as he did. The house of the Tobiads (from which Tobiah came) remained influential even in Maccabean times, 2 Maccabees 3:11.

Nehemiah's walls enclosed an area much smaller than that of preexilic Jerusalem. Even so, what mattered was that those walls encircled a city whose divine destiny had changed. It was no longer to serve as a symbol of the unity of north and south, or the seat of the Davidic dynasty, but as the center for preserving the unique worship of the new community.

Person in center of circle consisting of bricks, covenant, law–codes: After repairing Jerusalem's walls, Nehemiah made efforts to increase Jerusalem's population by having one tenth of Judah's citizens take up residence within its walls, Nehemiah 11:1,2.

5 Ezra—a scribe (Ezra 7:6), a descendant of Aaron (Ezra 7:1–5), and a Zadokite priest—accomplished several things among the exiles:

Symbol for law-code in circle around Judah and Jerusalem: When Ezra returned to Judah and Jerusalem, he brought with him the *Book of the Law* and read it to the members of the new community.

Symbol for covenant in the circle around Judah and Jerusalem: The people who listened to what Ezra read to them were deeply affected by what they heard and participated in a *covenant renewal ceremony*, Nehemiah 8.

 Male figure and symbol for Judaism; fragmentation symbol; female figure with two children; symbol for marriage, *lower right:* Although Nehemiah forbade any further marriages between Jewish men and Gentile women, he forced only one couple to separate. Ezra forbade all such marriages and insisted that Jewish men send away any Gentile wife and the children born of those unions. Ezra spoke of the Jews as a "holy seed" (or "people," Ezra 9:2) and accused the people of Judah of desecrating themselves with "the people of the land."

The issues at stake in Ezra's actions had to do with *spiritual*, *religious*, and *ethnic* purity. The ideals Ezra imposed on the postexilic community contributed greatly to that community's survival, and eventually enabled it to resist the attempted inroads of Hellenism.

The time came when Jewish religious leaders struggled with the question of the exclusion or inclusion of the Gentiles. Most rabbis favored the more exclusive strain found in Deuteronomy 23, Ezra, and Nehemiah. A very small number of rabbis embraced the position expressed in Isaiah 56:7, which stated that the Temple was to be a "house of prayer for all peoples."

 The contents of both Ezra and Nehemiah stress that Persian rulers showed concern for Judah and the returning exiles. The reason for this becomes more apparent when it is understood that Nehemiah's and Ezra's missions coincided with Egyptian revolts against Persian control. It was important for the Persians to have a sympathetic Judah behind their lines as they moved against a rebellious Egypt. Although Persian control of Judah made it impossible to reestablish the Davidic dynasty, Ezra supplied the postexilic community with another source of stability and continuity: a worship life centered around the Temple.

The Jewish *Talmud* considers Ezra to have been a second Moses (*Sanhedrin* 21b) because he restored observance of the Law. It claims that the Law would have been given through Ezra had Moses not preceded him. At the same time, Samaritan writings contain many negative comments about Ezra and cast him as the archenemy.

1 Cyrus' capture of Babylonia and its capital was greeted with joy, not only by the exiles, but also by many Babylonians. Cyrus demonstrated an enlightened policy toward conquered territories and peoples. He did not flatten cities, ravage shrines, pillage treasuries, and drag conquered nations into exile. Instead, he permitted conquered peoples to remain in their own territories, perpetuate national customs, and worship their own deities. Furthermore, he allowed exiles to return home and reestablish themselves. Cyrus' decree of liberation is recorded twice in Ezra (1:2–4 and 6:3–5). Both versions state that Cyrus gave the Jews permission to return to their homeland and decreed that Persian funds be provided to help rebuild the Jerusalem Temple, Ezra 6:4. The sacred vessels Nebuchadnezzar had taken from the Temple were to be returned, 1:7–11.

2 In 538 B.C., Cyrus entrusted the task of leading the first group of returning exiles back to Judah to Sheshbazzar, Ezra 1:5–11. It is possible that Sheshbazzar was a fourth son of Jehoiachin, 1 Chronicles 3:16–19 (Shenazzar). If so, he was the uncle of Zerubbabel, who led back a second group of exiles some years later, Ezra 3:2. Although a Jew, Sheshbazzar had a Babylonian name. We are not told what happened to him, or when he was replaced by Zerubbabel.

3 After the exiles arrived in Judah, Zerubbabel, and Joshua and fellow-priests, set up an altar in Jerusalem and installed Levites to officiate at it, Ezra 3:1–7. It is not clear which group of returning exiles put down the foundations. Ezra 3:2 says the altar was the work of the second group of returning exiles, while Ezra 5:16 says that Sheshbazzar laid the foundations of the new Temple. The first passage suggests that work on the foundations began in 520 B.C., while the second suggests an earlier date.

4 The new community was not free to operate at will; neighboring communities objected to their presence and caused them problems. Although the Babylonians had leveled most of Judah's towns to the ground in 587 B.C., they had left many poor people remaining in the land to harvest grapes and make wine. After all, the poor posed no threat to the ruling power. Many of these intermarried with foreigners brought in by the Babylonians to discourage and diffuse genetic and nationalistic loyalties. The Babylonians had also permitted many Edomites to settle in Hebron and other towns in southern Judah. These, and people who had taken up residence in Judah after the deportations, joined forces with the Samaritans to oppose and harass the returning exiles, hinder their building efforts, and make it difficult for them to reestablish themselves. The Samaritans in particular proved obnoxious. They insisted they had a right to take part in the building projects for they looked on themselves as loyal followers of the traditions of Moses. When Zerubbabel rejected their offers of help, the Samaritans' friendship gave way to hostility. They now did all they could to put an end to the new community's projects.

5 The Samaritans' reasons for acting as they did were not prompted solely by the Jewish refusal to let them get involved in the building projects. Economic and political factors also played a role. They feared the establishment of a separate Jewish state on their southern border and the renewal of Jewish nationalism that went with it. As a result, work on the Temple came to a halt for several years.

6 In 520 B.C., work on rebuilding the Temple resumed. The decision to recommence was made at a time when the Persian empire was plagued by political unrest; plot, counterplot, and murder had ravaged the royal court. Uprisings took place in the provinces. Eventually, Darius I managed to bring the situation under control. However, in about 521 B.C. a certain Nebuchadnezzar (*yes, the same name!*) spearheaded a revolt in Babylonia. Within a month, the Jewish community resumed building operations. Encouragement to complete the Temple was given by two prophets, Haggai and Zechariah.

7 Despite all opposition, the Temple was completed in 515 B.C. Zerubbabel then disappeared from the scene. How or why is not known. Some suggest that because he (a descendant of David) participated in a revolt against Persia incited from within Egypt about this time, the Persians killed him, fearing that his continued presence might fan the flames of nationalistic sentiment. No further mention is made of any attempt to revive the Davidic state during the Persian period. The High Priest and his successors became the leaders of the postexilic community, whose members saw themselves as a community of priests. They structured their mode of life on the pattern established (according to the Chronicler) by David himself.

8 The Old Testament contains virtually no information about the history of the Judean community immediately after the dedication of the Temple. The historical thread is taken up again at a later point in history in Ezra and Nehemiah. These two books confront the reader with the difficult problem of trying to establish a proper Ezra/Nehemiah chronology.

9 The writer (or editor) has put his materials together in a way that suggests Ezra did his work first, and Nehemiah did his later. However, the story of Ezra is preserved in Ezra 7–10 and Nehemiah 8–10, half in one book and half in the other. Many believe that Nehemiah did his work prior to Ezra. What follows is a suggested reconstruction of the various stages of the return from exile:

- A *first return* under Cyrus, about 538 B.C., led by Sheshbazzar.
- A *second return* under Darius I (521–485 B.C.), led by Joshua and Zerubbabel.
- A *third return* led by Nehemiah during the reign of Artaxerxes 1 (464–423 B.C.). Nehemiah made two visits to Jerusalem.
- A *fourth return* led by Ezra during the reign of Artaxerxes II (404–358 B.C.).

10 Both Ezra and Nehemiah hint that conditions in Judah after the completion of the Temple were far from satisfactory. There was need for reform and change. Change did come, but not from within the community.

11 In the Persian city of Susa, Nehemiah attained high office in the court of Artaxerxes I. He arranged for himself to be sent to Jerusalem with the commission to rebuild the city's ruined walls. There was real need for this since the city's inhabitants were being harassed by hostile neighbors, Nehemiah 1:1–2:8.

12 After arriving in Jerusalem, Nehemiah carried out a secret inspection of the ruined walls by night. He then set out to convince the people that their precarious situation would be greatly improved if they rebuilt the city's walls, 2:9–18. News of the plan reached the ears of the community's neighbors— in particular Sanballat, the governor of Samaria, and Tobiah, the governor of the Transjordan province, 2:10,19. These men made their opposition to the scheme very obvious, as did the governors of other neighboring provinces, Nehemiah 4:1f. Even so, with one hand on the trowel and the other on the sword (4:7–23), the Jews set to work to complete the project. When Sanballat and Tobiah heard that the project had been completed, they tried to lure Nehemiah out of the city to meet with them in a village on the plain of Ono; no doubt their goal was to do him harm. Nehemiah refused to meet with them, 6:1–9.

13 Nehemiah became aware that economic distress was plaguing some members of the community. Their plight was being aggravated by several factors. Although most were giving single-minded attention to repairing the city's walls, some of the more affluent in the community were charging their

less fortunate brothers interest on loans. Nehemiah took the lenders to task, and insisted that the situation be changed, 5:1–13. Furthermore, the loyalty of some within the community was not what it should have been; they were collaborating with foreign elements, 6:17–19.

 After the walls were repaired, Nehemiah turned his attention to problems of internal organization. From all localities in the province, he chose by lot one-tenth of the population and resettled those selected in Jerusalem, 7:4ff; 11:1ff. The list of names in ch. 7 indicates that this group was somewhat mixed; it contains Persian, Elamite, Moabite, and Jewish names, and refers to people from towns that had formerly been part of the Northern Kingdom—namely Jericho, Bethel, and Ai.

 After serving as governor for twelve years, Nehemiah returned to Susa about 433 B.C., but reappeared in Jerusalem some time later. Perhaps he had been informed about abuses still prevailing there, Nehemiah 13. Jews had been marrying women from Moab, Ammon, and Ashdod, 13:1–3, 23-27. The governor of Transjordan, Tobiah (who had "connections" with the priest Eliashib) had obtained the use of a room in the Temple, possibly for the practice of commerce, 13:4–9. Because the Levites and Temple singers were not being properly supported, they had to devote time to agricultural labors. As a result, they were forced to neglect their appointed duties, 13:10–14. Furthermore, the Sabbath was not being properly observed, 13:15–22.

 Nehemiah took action. He demanded that the people observe the following regulations:
- New mixed marriages were forbidden, 10:30.
- The Sabbath was to be observed properly, 10:31.
- Due attention was to be given to the payment of the Temple taxes, the provision of sacrifices (10:32–34), the offering of first fruits, and the payment of tithes, 10:35–38.

 It is not known how Nehemiah's career came to an end. He had devoted himself tirelessly to the improvement of the external conditions of the postexilic community, its cultic life, and its discipline. It was to be left to another to regulate the community's religious life: Ezra.

 Ezra's letter of appointment reveals something about his person and task, Ezra 7:11–26. He was a priest, "the scribe, a scholar of the text of the commandments of the Lord and his statutes for Israel," 7:11. He was commissioned to make an investigation of religious conditions in Jerusalem and Judah and was given permission to take with him any Jews who wished to return from Babylon to their homeland. He was also to take with him Persian subsidies for the Temple and gifts from the Babylonian Jews to purchase supplies for the regular sacrifices. Any additional sums needed for the Temple, up to a precisely fixed amount, were to be obtained from the official treasurer of the province. Finally, Ezra was to be responsible for the installation of judges as prescribed by Jewish religious law and for the instruction of those ignorant of Jewish teaching.

 Ezra began his work in Jerusalem on the first day of the seventh month by reading to the people from the writings he had brought with him from Babylon, "the book of the law of Moses," Nehemiah 8:1–12. Some suggest the book was the Pentateuch. The reading made a deep impression on the people. Because the hearers could no longer understand Hebrew, it was necessary for the Levites to translate the readings into Aramaic, the language the exiles had used in Babylon, Nehemiah 8:8. After the completion of the readings, the rest of the New Year's day was celebrated as a day of joy in the Lord. On the following day, the Feast of Tabernacles was observed. The scriptures were read again— this time to a smaller audience, Nehemiah 8:13–18.

Some believe that the ritual found in Nehemiah 8 served as a model for the synagogue service that developed in later Judaism (and is still practiced today): the bringing of the scroll, the mounting of the platform with the desk for reading, the opening of the scroll, the blessing, the communal "Amen."

 Nehemiah 9 suggests that a covenant renewal ceremony was held in connection with the observances led by Ezra. Prior to its observance, the Jews separated themselves from all foreigners and undertook a solemn confession of sins. The Scriptures were read. Ezra proclaimed words resembling the *Preamble* and *Historical Prologue* of a covenant formulation. The elements in the *Historical Prologue* list the creation, the patriarchal history, the Exodus, Sinai and wilderness events, the conquest, the destruction of Judah, and the exile, thus bringing the *Historical Prologue* up to date.

 Ezra also dealt with the continuing problem of mixed marriages in the community. He resorted to more drastic measures than did Nehemiah. He forced Jewish men to banish their Gentile wives and the children those wives had borne them, Ezra 9,10. Ezra acted as he did to establish within the community the dignity and holiness demanded by the Scriptures he had brought with him. He believed that only strict adherence to the Torah could ensure Israel's continued existence.

Haggai

1 When Cyrus proclaimed his decree of liberation in 538 B.C., there was not a general rush to return to Jerusalem. Many of the Jewish exiles had spent long years in Babylon. Many had been born there. Many had built themselves comfortable homes and established viable business ventures. Their roots went deep into Babylonian soil. They were loathe to undertake the long, difficult, and expensive journey back to Jerusalem. They preferred to leave it to others to make a new beginning to the nation's history in a poverty-stricken and insecure environment.

2 Haggai's message had bite and fire. He set out to stir a lethargic (as he saw it) Judean community into action. He pointed out that, in terms of economics, things were not going well in Judah. The people were busy building splendid houses for themselves but neglecting the rebuilding of the Temple. This was a bad state of affairs; the people needed to focus on something more important, 1:1–11.

3 Haggai's work bore fruit. The people supported Joshua and Zerubbabel and set to work with a will to rebuild the Temple, 1:12–15. However, the people became disillusioned because the new structure appeared to compare unfavorably with the preexilic Temple. Haggai dealt with their despondency by describing a vision of a Temple more grand than Solomon's had been. He assured them that God would become involved in their project in a striking way. God would shake the heavens, the earth, the sea, the dry land, and all nations, with the result that the treasures of the world would flow into the new Temple, 2:1–9. When it was completed, the people would enjoy abundant prosperity, 2:15–19.

4 The book closes with a veiled reference to Zerubbabel as God's Messiah, 2:20–23. In doing so, it uses Exodus terminology to describe God's coming victory over Israel's foes, 2:22.

Zechariah

Zechariah 1–8 was written about the same time as Haggai. Chs. 9–14 contain a number of difficult, obscure references and apparently come from a later period.

Zechariah 1-8

The opening chapters employ a literary form different from prophetic writings previously encountered. The prophet presents his message in the form of a series of night visions with dialogue between the Lord, the prophet, and an interpreting angel. In each vision:

- The prophet sees something;
- The prophet asks about what he has seen;
- The prophet is given an explanation by the angel.

Each vision ends with a statement about good things to come.

Zechariah reminds the people that, because they ignored the teachings and warnings of the prophets, the exile resulted, 1:1–6. He urges the postexilic community not to walk in the ways of their ancestors, but to prepare themselves for the coming Messianic Age.

1 *In the first vision* (1:7–17), the prophet sees four horsemen whose duty it is to patrol the earth for the Lord. They report that, although all is peaceful among the nations, Judah's miserable lot remains unchanged. The assurance is given that Jerusalem and the Temple will be rebuilt and that the cities of the land will enjoy great prosperity. God expresses anger at those nations who have harmed Israel and hints that they will be punished.

2 *In the second vision* (1:18–21), the prophet sees four horns. These represent the nations that have inflicted sufferings on Israel and Judah. He also sees four blacksmiths, representing the agents God will use to overthrow those guilty nations prior to the breaking in of the Messianic Age.

3 *In the third vision* (2:1–5), the prophet sees a man measuring the dimensions of the New Jerusalem. He is told that the city will be of great size to cope with the expected number of inhabitants. The city will not need walls, for God will guarantee its safety.

The section that follows (2:6–13), contains an appeal to the exiles. It states that God will overcome those nations that have been keeping God's people in subjection. The Israelites are urged to flee from Babylon and return to Judah. God will take up residence in the Temple. People from many nations will flock to Jerusalem to dwell there and become God's people also.

4 *In the fourth vision* (3:1–10), Joshua, the High Priest, stands before the angel of the Lord. Satan stands beside Joshua to accuse him, but Satan's accusations are rejected. Joshua had been clothed in filthy garments; the reference is to the sin and guilt, not only of Joshua, but of the whole community. However, their sin and guilt are taken away. Purification is a necessary prelude to the coming Messianic era. Joshua and his fellow-priests are assured that they will have direct access to the heavenly courts with their prayers on behalf of Jerusalem. The term "Branch" in v. 8 is a Messianic title. Here it refers to a person other than Joshua, most likely Zerubbabel. In 3:10 the blessings of the coming Messianic Age are described in familiar terms, Micah 4:4; 1 Kings 4:25.

5 *In the fifth vision* (4:1–14), the prophet sees a golden lamp stand and two olive trees. Emphasis is placed on the two olive trees. These either supply oil for the seven lamps on the lamp stand, or merely

flank them. The olive trees represent Zerubbabel and Joshua, God's specially consecrated agents in the postexilic community. With the help of God's Spirit, Zerubbabel is to complete the work of rebuilding the Temple, 4:6–10. This task is of great significance, for God will grant the blessings of the New Age from His dwelling place in the Jerusalem Temple. The completion of the Temple is a necessary prelude to the Messianic Age.

6   *In the sixth vision* (5:1–4), the prophet sees an immense flying scroll which represents God's curse on sinners. The curse banishes and destroys all sin—a necessary prelude to the Messianic Age.

7   *In the seventh vision* (5:5–11), the prophet sees a woman in a measuring container. She represents the sin which must be removed from the Holy Land as a prelude to the coming Messianic Age. Sin is personified as a female deity who is to be taken to a Babylonian temple to be worshiped there.

8   *The eighth vision* (6:1–8) contains a number of details (four chariot horses and two mountains of bronze) the meaning of which is uncertain. Possibly the reference is to the breaking in of the Messianic Age with its accompanying judgment of all the earth.

9   *The next section* (6:9–15) bristles with difficulties. It is possible that originally it gave directions concerning the crowning of Zerubbabel as Messianic king, but for some reason the name of Joshua was substituted. Some suggest that both names should be included, and that the word "crown" should be "crowns." The general thrust of vv. 12–15 is that Zerubbabel will complete the building of the Temple, a task in which he will be helped by exiles God will bring back to Jerusalem. The High Priest will assist Zerubbabel in the task of overseeing the Messianic community. King and priest are to work side by side in the management of the affairs of the postexilic community.

10   Chapter 7 deals with an inquiry about whether or not the practice of observing a fast to commemorate the destruction of the Temple in 587 B.C. should be continued. The answer echoes the emphases of preexilic prophets.

11   Chapter 8 contains many Messianic assurances.

    a.   God will dwell on Mt. Zion among the people, v. 3.

    b.   God will bring back those scattered among the nations, vv. 7,8.

    c.   The covenant bond will be restored, v. 8.

    d.   God will bless the people, vv. 9–15.

    e.   People of many other nations will come to Jerusalem to seek the Lord, v. 13, vv. 20–23; see also Genesis 12:1–3, Isaiah 2:2–4.

    f.   The pursuit of righteousness will be the concern of all, vv. 16,17.

    g.   Fast days will become joyous liturgical feast days, vv. 18,19 (these verses seem to answer the question raised in the previous chapter).

    h.   The community is called "the remnant," a term with Messianic significance, vv. 6,11,12; see also Haggai 1:12.

Zechariah 9–14

1   These chapters contain two collections of oracles, beginning at 9:1 and 12:1 respectively. The interpretation of these chapters is the subject of continuing debate. It is difficult to determine the situation to which they originally spoke.

2. Some of the motifs in this section play an important role in the Gospel narratives. Note the following parallels:

   a. *The king is coming:* Zechariah 9:9 and John 12:14,15.

   b. *Thirty pieces of silver:* Zechariah 11:12,13 and Matthew 27:3–10.

   c. *The pierced one:* Zechariah 12:10 and John 19:33–37.

   d. *The smitten shepherd:* Zechariah 13:7–9 and Mark 14:26–31.

   e. *The cleansing of the Temple:* Zechariah 14:21b and John 2:16.

3. In Zechariah 9:9, the hope is that the Davidic and Solomonic kingdom will be restored, but by one who will avoid the arrogance of the monarchy (symbolized by chariots and horses). After all, the postexilic community would not need weapons and armies because God would kill their enemies for them. The role of the people was to maintain purity and be obedient to the law.

4. The allegory of sheep and shepherds in Zechariah 11 is a difficult one. In the ancient world, shepherds represented kings and rulers; see Ezekiel 34. The prophet attacks the rulers who exploit the people. Although the prophet is assigned to shepherd the people for a time, the people do not heed him, and are given over to a foolish shepherd who takes no care of them. The wage of the prophet is the price of a slave, which is the value that sheep merchants (foreign powers) attach to the God of Israel; see also Matthew 26:15. The two staffs in Zechariah 11 symbolize two covenants: one with the nations, and the other between Judah and Israel. Both are broken in the course of the prophecy, thus reversing Ezekiel's prediction of salvation (Ezekiel 37). John 10 contains Jesus' final word on this matter.

5. The theme that runs through Zechariah 12–14 is that of a final battle in Jerusalem. The traditional view was that, in the last days, all nations would assemble to fight against Mt. Zion, Psalm 2; Ezekiel 38,39. Chs. 12–14 suggest that there was tension between Judah and Jerusalem, and that Judah must be saved first lest Jerusalem gloat over it.

   a. In ch. 12, the emphasis is on reconciliation between the two. Jerusalem and the Davidic house will be compassionate and will "look on the one whom they have pierced," 12:10. This statement has given rise to endless speculation. What is clear is that the prophet looked for a time when the leaders in Jerusalem would show compassion to the people they had oppressed, and would be reconciled with them.

   b. In ch. 14, the prophet envisages reconciliation between Judah and the nations, so that even the Egyptians will come to Jerusalem to celebrate the Feast of Tabernacles.

1 As a result of Ezra's work, the spirit of legalism surfaced and developed. The term does not imply that postexilic Jews thought they were made right with God by keeping the law-codes of the Pentateuch. They knew that behind the law-codes stood the Law-Giver—the gracious God who had rescued the Israelites from Egypt. The consensus was that everything of value had already been delivered to Moses. All that mattered, then, was that the Mosaic writings be preserved, studied, interpreted, and applied. This concern for the *many minute details of the written scriptures* is defined as *legalism*. However, with the passing of time some rabbis embraced the notion that they and God's people could manipulate God through obedience to the law-codes.

2 The meaning of the term "legalism" becomes more obvious if the term *Torah* or *Law* is defined. It means instruction, teaching, revelation. Jews apply the term in a broad sense to all their sacred writings, more narrowly to the Old Testament, and specifically to the Pentateuch (Genesis through Deuteronomy). The term can also be used to refer to the law-codes embedded within the Pentateuch, but its general application is broader than this. If, then, the term *Torah* or *Law* is understood to refer to the Old Testament writings, it is easier to understand that *legalism* proceeded from the premise that all necessary truth was contained within those writings. The challenge was to study, understand, systematize, and codify that truth.

3 Admittedly, Judaism did develop certain weaknesses because of this emphasis on legalism. Temple rituals often became empty displays—done for their own sake. Some manipulated the interpretation of the law-codes to water down God's will for their lives. A policy of exclusiveness developed in the minds of some with respect to those who did not have the Hebrew scriptures.

4 Even among the Jews themselves, some claimed the right to decide who was of God and who was not of God. Often the deciding factor was whether the person under scrutiny paid sufficient attention to such external observances as the Sabbath and circumcision.

5 Isaiah spoke of God's coming rescue of the exiles from Babylon as a Second Exodus, 43:14–21; 51:9–11. The conviction emerged that any person wishing to belong to the new community must have taken part in the return from Babylon or have descended from someone who had done so. This belief gave rise to a concern for racial purity and family lineage, Ezra 2:59,62,63. It also explains what lies behind the remarks of John the Baptist in Matthew 3:9,10.

6 Postexilic legalism resulted in a decrease in the spirit and fire of prophecy. True, names such as Haggai, Zechariah, Obadiah, Malachi, and Joel remind us that there were some prophets at work beyond 538 B.C. However, these individuals were of a lesser breed than those who worked before and during the exile—prophets like Amos, Hosea, Isaiah, Micah, Jeremiah, and Ezekiel.

As time went by, the prophetic movement became increasingly discredited and was viewed with suspicion. There were reasons for this. The predictions concerning the glorious restoration after the exile did not come to pass. There was conflict among the prophets themselves. Some were willing to mislead the people for the sake of personal gain, 1 Kings 22; Jeremiah 28:1–4. In Zechariah 13:3, even a prophet's parents were to assume that any oracle their son spoke in the name of the Lord was a lie. There came the day when visionaries of the Maccabean period used pen-names and attributed their oracles to ancient heroes such as Daniel and Enoch.

33A They then began work on rebuilding the Temple itself. Although work on the project suffered some delays (e.g., because of the people's poverty), eventually the project was completed and the new structure was dedicated in 515 B.C. The prophets Haggai and Zechariah played a role in encouraging the new community to complete the project.

Efforts to rebuild Jerusalem itself gained momentum after Nehemiah spearheaded the move to rebuild the city's walls. After the project was completed, Nehemiah arranged for more Jews to take up residence behind those walls.

After Ezra returned, he reinstated and revitalized the role of covenant within the life of the community. Both he and Nehemiah took steps to remove non-Jewish elements and people from the community, insisting that Jewish men enter into a marriage relationship only with Jewish women. Gentile wives, and the children sired by their Jewish husbands, were sent away.

33B The members of the restored community were not free to operate at will. They had to deal with opposition from the Judeans who had not been taken into exile, from the Edomites to the east (who had moved into the land after helping the Babylonians in their campaign in 587 B.C.), and from the Samaritans to the north. The Old Testament writings contain little information about what transpired between the rededication of the Temple in 515 B.C. and the return of Nehemiah and Ezra from Babylon. Among other things, Nehemiah found himself having to deal with the exploitation of the poor by the rich and affluent.

33C The prophet Haggai set out to stir into action a lethargic Judean community that was focusing on building lavish homes for themselves but neglecting the rebuilding of the Temple. Even so, many felt disillusioned because they feared that the new structure would compare unfavorably with Solomon's Temple. Haggai responded by assuring the people that God was doing things that would result in the wealth of the world flowing into the new structure—and the people themselves would eventually enjoy abundant prosperity.

33D Zechariah 1–8 were written about the same time as Haggai. Six visions surface within these chapters—visions that, among other things, assure the members of the restored community that Jerusalem and the Temple will be rebuilt, that they themselves will soon enjoy great prosperity, and that any nation that has made life difficult for them will be punished. Ch. 8 contains many messianic assurances. It is difficult to determine when chs. 9–14 were written, and what situations they address. The central theme in chs. 12–14 has to do with a final battle in Jerusalem in the last days—a battle when all nations would unite to fight against Mt. Zion.

33E Ezra focused on preserving, studying, interpreting, and applying the Torah—Genesis through Deuteronomy. Eventually, the notion developed that God's people could manipulate and influence God through obedience to the law-codes. This spirit of legalism resulted in a neglect of the prophetic writings, and a concern for genetic purity and external rituals.

CROSS WAYS®

4
SECTION

UNITS 31–40

The Postexilic Period and Judaism

UNIT 34

Malachi, Joel, Ruth, Jonah, Esther

The Central Message of the Books Listed

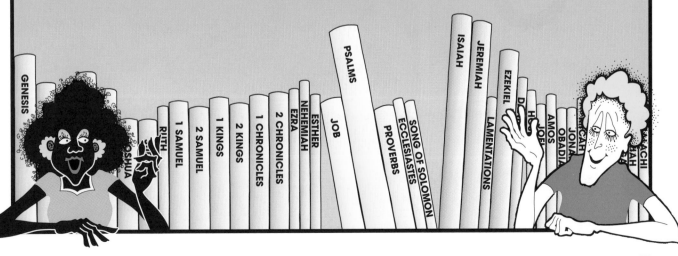

ILLUSTRATION

34A

© H. N. Wendt 2007

42

BOAZ **(RUTH)** OBED

JESSE

1

2

3

4

5

1 Malachi

Prophetic figure; hourglass, with the sands of time nearly run out: Malachi stressed the nearness of the Day of the Lord. God would send Elijah to prepare the people for its coming.

2 Joel

Locusts; hourglass, with the sands of time nearly run out: Joel also spoke of the soon-to-come Day of the Lord. He made reference to a plague of locusts that had been ravaging the countryside, and saw in it a sign from God to alert the nation to the imminent appearance of that Day.

3 Ruth

Family line; crown, with Star of David: Although numerous suggestions are made concerning why Ruth was written, any book that made reference to David's family line would have been deemed worthy of preservation. The book describes the preservation of Elimelech's family line, and notes that David was a descendant of Ruth and Boaz.

4 Jonah

Unhappy Jonah beneath a tree; Nineveh skyline: Jonah was sent to exhort the people of Nineveh to repent, and to his surprise and disappointment, they repented. The final chapter depicts Jonah sitting beneath a tree God had provided to supply shade. When the tree withered and Jonah lost his shade, he became as upset as he had been when Nineveh repented. The story was designed to show that although the Lord had shown mercy to the Israelites, they were not ready to show mercy to other nations. They longed for the day to come when God would destroy the Gentiles.

5 Esther

Hangman's noose; face: Esther describes how Jews in Persia foiled a plot, devised by an official named Haman, to destroy them and turned the tables on their enemies. The gallows that Haman (a *Persian* official) designed for the execution of Mordecai (a *Jew*) became the instrument on which Haman himself was put to death.

1 The name Malachi means "my messenger," 3:1. The book deals with issues that indicate when it was written. Malachi's literary structure is unique. It consists of six sections. Each section begins with a statement and a question, and explanations of the theme.

> *You have wearied the Lord with your words.*
>   *Yet you say, 'How have we wearied him?'*
> *By saying,*
>   *'All who do evil are good in the sight of the Lord, and he delights in them.'*
> *Or by asking,*
>   *'Where is the God of justice?'* (2:17)

The verses that follow (3:1ff) declare that God will indeed judge, and that this judgment will be like a refiner's fire. No one will be able to endure God's coming.

2 The six sections are:

a. **1:1–5:** God's love for Jacob is greater than God's love for Esau. This section does not contain any reproach of Israel. All other sections do.

b. **1:6–2:9:** Both the priests and the laity are withholding honor from the Lord.

c. **2:10–16:** Jewish men have been marrying foreign women and practicing their pagan worship rituals. These men are faithless to the Lord.

d. **2:17–3:5:** The people have questioned God's justice. God will judge them for this!

e. **3:6–12:** The people are robbing God by withholding the tithes due to Him.

f. **3:13–4:3:** Many in the community neglect their duty to worship. Some even despise worship. There are, however, some who are faithful. They will be rewarded.

3 Worship life in the Temple was at a low ebb. Worshipers thought that they could offer blemished animals in their sacrifices, 1:7,8,13. Malachi lays the blame for this indifference at the feet of the leaders of the people, especially the priests, 2:1–3,8,9. Many in the community flippantly declared that it made more sense to be irreligious than religious, for it paid a better dividend. Malachi described the priests as ignorant, indulgent, and grasping, and felt compelled to attack them. The references to abuses in the Temple, divorce and mixed marriages, and exploitation of the poor by the rich, indicate that Malachi was written about 500–450 B.C., possibly before the arrival of Nehemiah and Ezra.

4 Malachi repeats Obadiah's threat of impending disaster for the Edomites, 1:3–5. Some interpret his reference to widespread, acceptable Gentile worship quite literally. Others relate it to the expected Messianic Age when the sacrifices offered by all the nations would be acceptable to the Lord, 1:11. The prophet describes the ideal priest (2:5–7), and lists the blessings the obedient Israelites could expect to receive, 3:10–12,16,17. In 4:2,3, reference is made to a separation of the righteous from the unrighteous taking place already in this life. The names of those who feared the Lord were being recorded in a book; they would be spared on the Day of Judgment, 3:16–18.

5 Malachi concludes with a prediction that the Lord would send Elijah to summon Israel to repentance, and to prepare the people for the great and terrible Day of the Lord, 3:1–4; 4:5,6; see also Matthew 11:10–14; 17:10–13; Mark 1:2; 6:14,15; Luke 1:17,76; 7:27.

Joel

1 Little is known about Joel, the son of Pethuel, or when he did his work. The writing does not mention any reigning king. Elders and priests occupy the prominent positions in the community, 1:2,13; 2:17. Judah is called Israel, indicating that the northern tribes no longer exist, 2:27. The destruction of Jerusalem, the exile, and the annexation of Jewish territory are but memories, 3:1–3,17. The community Joel addresses occupies only a small amount of territory; it is virtually within earshot of a trumpet blast from the Temple, 1:14; 2:1,15,16. Although the exile is over, some Jews are still scattered among the nations, 3:2. To add to the problems of the postexilic community, the Phoenicians and Philistines have sold off some of its members as slaves to the Greeks, 3:6.

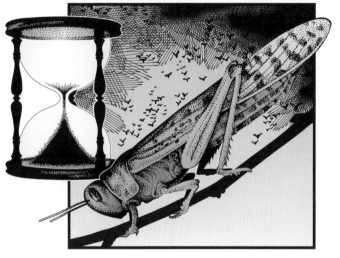

2 Joel, like Malachi and Obadiah, depicts a struggling postexilic community facing threats from neighboring nations and their cultures, and weakened within by poverty, discontent, and spiritual indifference. These factors move some scholars to suggest that Joel was written about the time of Malachi—possibly a little later. Others date it after the time of Nehemiah and Ezra—a time when the restored remnant had rallied around the Temple, made the study of the Law its focal point, and settled down to await the Day of the Lord.

3 Joel spoke at a time when the land was being ravaged by a plague of locusts (described as an invading army), and the people were terror-stricken, 1:1–2:17. Joel said the plague was more than a passing phenomenon of nature; it heralded the Day of the Lord. The locusts' march across the land should arouse within the people a holy fear of the Lord's power. Accordingly, Joel urged the people to engage in intense prayer. Joel's message had the desired effect. The people gave themselves over to repentance and prayer. Joel did not stop there. He assured the people that the Day was approaching when God's spirit would be poured out on all flesh (i.e., all in *Israel*). Furthermore, just as the plague would soon be dispersed, so too harassing nations would be destroyed on that Day when God would intervene decisively on behalf of His people. Judah would then flourish again, 2:18–27.

4 Joel makes use of apocalyptic imagery:
- The outpouring of the spirit of prophecy, 2:28,29.
- Cataclysmic changes in the sun, moon, and earth, 2:30–32.
- The assembling of the nations in the valley of Jehoshaphat ("the Lord judges") for judgment, 3:2,12.
- The flowing of a healing stream from the Temple in Jerusalem, 3:18 (see also Ezekiel 47:1–12 and Zechariah 13:1).

5 Joel is best remembered by Christians for how Peter quoted him in his Pentecost sermon, Acts 2:17–21 (see Joel 2:28); the reference in both contexts is to "all Israel"—to all *Jews*. The *Gentile* Pentecost is reported in Acts 10.

Ruth

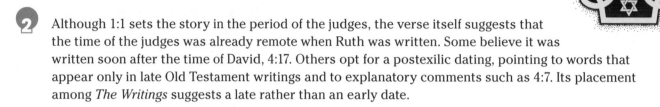

BOAZ **(RUTH)** → OBED → JESSE

1 The narrative is set in the period of the Judges (1:1), hence its location in English Bibles. In the Hebrew Bible, Ruth is placed among *The Writings* where it is the second of the *Megilloth* (the *Five Scrolls*: Song of Solomon, Ruth, Lamentations, Ecclesiastes, and Esther). It is read as part of the Jewish liturgy for Pentecost, the festival that celebrates both harvest and the giving of the Law on Mt. Sinai. The author is unknown.

2 Although 1:1 sets the story in the period of the judges, the verse itself suggests that the time of the judges was already remote when Ruth was written. Some believe it was written soon after the time of David, 4:17. Others opt for a postexilic dating, pointing to words that appear only in late Old Testament writings and to explanatory comments such as 4:7. Its placement among *The Writings* suggests a late rather than an early date.

3 In ancient Israel (as in other peoples of that time) a strong sense of family solidarity existed. A man had sons and, thereby, a clan, a family. Each member of the clan was considered an extension of the original patriarch. The good name and continuity of the clan was the concern of all. Furthermore, a man's fields, house, and possessions were extensions of himself. Loss of these threatened the continuity and vitality of the clan. The custom was, therefore, that whenever a poor kinsman was forced to sell or lose his property, another kinsman had to intervene to keep the property in the clan. He did this by buying it himself or redeeming it from the outsider who had taken it, Leviticus 25:25; see also Jeremiah 32:6–9.

The continuity and integrity of the clan was also threatened by childlessness. A man perpetuated his name and memory through sons and grandsons. If he died without sons, he died completely, and the life of the clan came to an end. There was a way in which this could be averted. The man's brother was obliged to marry his deceased brother's widow. The first son of the new union was considered the son of the deceased, the heir to his property, and the one who sustained the name and line of the deceased brother, Deuteronomy 25:5,6.

4 The punch-line of Ruth occurs in 4:17: "They named him Obed; he became the father of Jesse, the father of David." The fruit of the marriage of Ruth and Boaz was Obed, David's grandfather. A short genealogy appears in 4:18–22; see also 1 Chronicles 2:3–17. This information about David's family tree was more than enough to warrant the book's preservation. It is unlikely that David's genetic links to the Moabites would have been concocted.

There is more. The author gently stresses Ruth's Moabite background (1:4,22; 2:2,6,21) and hints that God accomplishes divine purposes through events in the unspectacular, everyday lives of God's people. Furthermore, David's connection with Moab would explain why he took his parents to Moab for safekeeping after Saul turned against him, 1 Samuel 22:3,4.

5 Other reasons for writing Ruth have been suggested. Some believe it was written to counteract the stern decrees of Nehemiah and Ezra that required Jewish men to divorce their Gentile wives and marry only women of their own race. The argument of the book, then, would be that surely marriage to a Gentile woman need not always be a bad thing. Indeed, even David had a Moabitess in his family tree. This view has its weak point, for the story might just as well have been used to *support* the measures taken in the reforms of Nehemiah and Ezra. After all, Ruth was a Moabitess who gave up her country and her gods to *become an exemplary adherent of the God of Israel!*

6 Others simply include Ruth among those Old Testament stories that show how God acted to preserve descendants of Abraham in the face of difficulties. It was often a woman who played the central role in these events: Sarah, Genesis 15:3, 16:1; Rebekah, Genesis 25:21; Rachel, Genesis 30:1,2; Lot's daughters, Genesis 19:30–38; Tamar, Genesis 38; see also Judges 13:1–25; 1 Samuel 1:2. In some of these narratives, the issue at stake is the preservation of the family line. Ruth focuses its attention on a similar crisis: "Will the line of Elimelech continue?"

7 Several of these emphases in Ruth may be woven together to show how a strategically important family (for the history of Israel) escaped extinction, and to point out that David himself was born as a result. The main characters are courtly in the way they speak and act, and are well worthy of emulation. Perhaps the writer also wanted to rekindle among the people of God an increased awareness of their great privilege and responsibility. Although they had received a glorious revelation from God (which needed to be kept free from the polluting influences of paganism), they also had to share that revelation with all—with even a Moabite woman.

1. Jonah is one of the best-known stories in the Bible. Some identify Jonah with the prophet mentioned in 2 Kings 14:25 and interpret the book as an historical narrative. However, the majority of scholars today believe Jonah is a postexilic story designed to make a moral and religious point.

2. The man Jonah is referred to in a satirical tone. It is unlikely that an actual prophet would have written about himself this way. If anything, Jonah acts like an *anti-prophet* whose behavior is the opposite of what might be expected from a prophet. Some of the details of the story are almost humorous. The idea that one can get away from the presence of the Lord by sailing to a remote place is ridiculous. The pagan sailors show more respect for God than does Jonah. When Jonah finally preaches in Nineveh, the Assyrians repent with unparalleled fervor. Even the animals join in the repentance process.

   Furthermore, significant details in the story are lacking, such as the name of the land where the fish deposited Jonah, and the name of the king of Nineveh. Some of the Hebrew words used suggest a date later than the eighth century. The mentality of the author is of the fifth rather than of the eighth century B.C. These factors suggest the writer was not writing about events of his own time and experience.

3. Ezra, Nehemiah, and Ruth indicate that, in the postexilic period, there was considerable interest in Israel's relationship to other nations. Most likely this issue forms the background for the message of Jonah. It speaks to the negative attitude of those Jews who longed for the *destruction* of their enemies rather than for their *salvation* (an attitude that prevails throughout the book of Nahum). The author wants to teach a pointed lesson about the limitless nature of the Lord's mercy and grace. The book, then, might be understood as a teaching story with a profound theological purpose. This explains why it lacks details of geography, chronology, history, and topography, why it contains certain grotesque elements such as the fish and the plant, and why it ends so abruptly after it has made its moral point. The book says nothing about the history of Nineveh beyond Jonah's ministry, nor does it say anything about Jonah's continuing ministry.

4. The book falls naturally into two parts. In the first two chapters, Jonah, himself a Jew, benefits from the Lord's mercy. In chs. 3 and 4, Jonah begrudges God's readiness to lavish that same mercy on others, specifically on non-Jews. The book may be outlined as follows:

   a. **Chapter 1:** The Lord sends Jonah to the Assyrian city of Nineveh to urge its inhabitants to repent. However, Jonah does not want to go anywhere near that infamous city; it has made life difficult for the Jewish people. So, he boards a ship bound for Tarshish, possibly the city of Tartesson in Spain. (A Jew would have looked on Tarshish as situated at the farthest limits of the world.) Apparently Jonah believes God's presence is confined to the territory in which His worshipers reside. God interferes with Jonah's plan. He whips up a storm that threatens the safety of the ship and all on board. Jonah sleeps through it all! Eventually, the crew members single out Jonah as the one responsible for their predicament.

Jonah's confession is ironic, 1:9. Although he declares that his God made the sea and the dry land, he thinks that he can escape from God's presence. Jonah is inconsistent, v. 12. He is willing to sacrifice himself so that the sailors might be spared, but later is anything but humane in his attitude toward the Ninevites. At this point, Jonah does not repent of his actions; he merely sees how futile they are. So, Jonah goes over the side into the deep. All is not lost. He is swallowed by a great fish, whose belly becomes his home for three days and three nights, v. 17.

b.   **Chapter 2:** Jonah prays a psalm of thanksgiving to the Lord for his deliverance. Although Jonah is in the belly of a fish, he has received abundant mercy from God. His life has been saved! Eventually, he is spewed up on a nameless coastline, v. 10.

c.   **Chapter 3:** The word of the Lord comes to Jonah a second time and sets him on the road to Nineveh once again. This time Jonah obeys and arrives at the assigned destination. He finds Nineveh to be a large city. He preaches to the city's residents (v. 4) and exhorts them to repent, not because of any change of heart in him, but because God has commanded him to do this. The last thing Jonah hopes is that Nineveh will repent. But *Nineveh does repent*, vv. 5–9! God spares the city and its people, 3:10.

d.   **Chapter 4:** Jonah should be overcome with joy about the outcome of his preaching, but he is not. He is so angry and resentful that he asks God to take his life, v. 3. God refuses to grant Jonah's request. The situation is pathetic and ludicrous. From God's point of view, Jonah's mission was a huge success. From Jonah's point of view it was a failure. He did not want those Ninevites to repent. He wanted God to pour His divine wrath on them. So Jonah takes up a position to the east of the city, and waits to see if that wrath might still come.

The details of the story become a little confusing in 4:5,6. The first of these two verses says that Jonah had access to a tent for shade. The second says that God caused a plant to grow near Jonah to provide shade. Jonah is happy about the plant. The next day God sends a worm that attacks the plant and causes it to wither. Jonah is left with no protection from sun or wind. He is most uncomfortable and again asks God to let him die, v. 8. God again refuses to comply and rebukes Jonah. The rebuke sums up the message of the book:

> *Jonah, you are very upset about that plant. However, it cost you no effort and no pain. You did not cultivate it. It grew up overnight and faded overnight. What about My right to have feelings for the people of Nineveh? Should I not be concerned about this teeming city? You showed concern for something that lived for a short time. Do I not have a right to feel great mercy for people, for even the least intelligent of human beings, and for beasts, all of whom are of much more value than a mere plant?*

5   The point is made. The writer satirizes those narrow-minded Israelites who had long experienced God's mercy, but begrudged that mercy to others. In the postexilic period, many in Israel prayed that God would pour out divine wrath on those nations that had made life difficult for them. This short book of four chapters cries out for a more merciful attitude.

1 The book of Esther is one of the five scrolls that Jews continue to read when important Jewish festivals are observed. (Esther is read during the observance of *Purim.*) The Hebrew version does not contain any reference to God or to the religious customs of Judaism. Several passages have been added to the Greek version of the book to give it a more spiritual tone. Esther eventually came to be regarded as second in importance only to the Pentateuch itself. Its manuscripts exceed in number those of any other book of the Bible, and are often magnificently illuminated and encased in silver and gold of exquisite workmanship.

2 The story is set in the reign of Ahasuerus (also known as Xerxes I) who reigned 486–465 B.C. The scene is Xerxes' winter palace in Susa. The king had prepared a lavish banquet, but his queen Vashti refused to put in an appearance and was deposed, 1:10–21). The king ordered a search throughout the empire for beautiful women, so that he might choose one of them as his new queen, 2:2–4. A Jewish lass, Hadassah— called Esther in the book—took part in the competition. She was so beautiful that it was not even necessary for her to go through the customary one year of beauty treatment to win the king's heart, 2:5–18.

3 Esther's cousin, Mordecai, served on the staff at the king's palace. When he learned of a plot to kill the king, he shared the secret with Esther, who in turn alerted the king. The plotters were put to death, 2:19–23. However, Mordecai ran into trouble with Xerxes' grand vizier, Haman, because Mordecai refused to pay him the appropriate courtesies. Haman so resented Mordecai's attitude that he devised a plot to destroy all Jews within the Persian empire, 3:1–6. He pointed out to the king that the Jews refused to assimilate, and chose to live by their own laws, 3:8. Xerxes permitted him to issue an edict stating that all Jews were to be massacred on the 13th day of the month of Adar.

It is known that the Jews achieved positions of wealth and influence throughout the Persian Empire— which probably resulted in hostility among the Gentiles. Haman paid Xerxes 10,000 talents (one and a quarter tons) of silver for permission to exploit or destroy the Jews.

4 To deal with the threat, Mordecai persuaded Esther to risk her life in order to save her people, ch. 4. She appeared before the king in an unsummoned visit—even though such an action could be punished by death. She asked that both the king and Haman take part in a banquet that she herself would prepare for them that very day, 5:1–8. They did this. She invited them to dine with her again the next day. On his way home, Haman saw Mordecai—and was filled with anger towards him. Haman's wife and friends suggested that he set up a huge gallows and ask the king to have Mordecai hanged on it, 5:9–14.

5 Fortunately, that very night the king remembered that Mordecai had saved his life but had never been rewarded. The next day, when Haman went to Xerxes to persuade him to have Mordecai hanged, he found himself being sent by Xerxes to honor Mordecai, ch. 6.

6 When Haman returned to the palace to join the royal couple in the second banquet, he became horrified when Esther poured out her heart to the king about the approaching slaughter of her people and laid the blame for the plot at Haman's feet, ch. 7. The king moved away to ponder the situation, and Haman pleaded with Esther for his life. The king interpreted Haman's action as an attempted assault on the queen and had him hanged on the gallows he had prepared for Mordecai, 7:10. Haman's ten sons were also put to death and his property was handed over to Esther. Mordecai was entrusted with the position left vacant by Haman's execution.

7. Haman had plotted to have all Jews put to death on the 13th day of Adar. Instead, the Jews in Susa were given permission to put their persecutors to death on that day, ch. 8. The Jews who lived out in the provinces were permitted to do the same thing on the 14th day of Adar, 9:5–10. When this "holy war" was over, a joyous celebration was held. This festival came to be known as *Purim*, to recall the lot (in Hebrew, *Pur*) Haman had cast to decide on which day the Jews were to be slaughtered, 9:18–23. The book explains the reason for the celebration of Purim and why it was celebrated on two days, 3:7; ch. 9.

8. The book of Esther would have spoken meaningfully to Jews being subjected to persecution because of their refusal to assimilate. The account of the origin of *Purim* (9:18,19) came to mean much to the Jews during the Maccabean period. According to the Jewish Talmud, it is permissible to drink wine during *Purim* until the difference between "Blessed be Mordecai!" and "Cursed be Haman!" becomes blurred and indistinguishable. Perhaps this explains why the name of God is not mentioned in Esther, lest it be uttered during *Purim* in an inappropriate manner.

9. According to 3:1, Haman was a descendant of Agag. Agag was king of the Amalekites whom King Saul was sent to annihilate, 1 Samuel 15. The Amalekites were remembered as the most dangerous of Israel's enemies, Exodus 17:14; Deuteronomy 25:17–19; 1 Samuel 27:8–12, 30:1–20. Perhaps the point is that although Saul wanted to spare the life of this enemy of Israel, Mordecai made no such mistake concerning Haman (Esther 7:9,10), and his fellow Jews should do the same when dealing with those who oppose them.

34A Joel, Jonah, and Malachi find a place in the prophetic writings. The Hebrew Bible places Ruth and Esther among The Writings.

34B Malachi spoke to a disillusioned, spiritually lethargic, postexilic community. Although he speaks of God's great love for the people of Judah, he rebukes:

- The priests and laity for failing to honor the Lord;
- Jewish men for marrying Gentile women and worshiping their gods;
- The people for questioning God's justice;
- The people for robbing God by withholding their tithes;
- Those who neglect their duty to worship—and even despise worship.

Malachi reminded the people of the approach of the Day of the Lord and urged all to walk in the ways of obedience. He declared that God would send Elijah to prepare the people for the coming of that great and terrible Day.

34C Joel, like Malachi, had much to say about the coming of the Day of the Lord. He used the tragic occurrence of a plague of locusts to urge the people to repent and prepare for that Day. When it came, God would judge those nations that had been harassing the members of the postexilic community and would pour out His spirit on all in Israel. The Day would not come unannounced but would be heralded by signs of the sun, moon, and earth, and by the return of Elijah. When the Day finally came, the mountains of Judah would flow with wine, the hills with milk, the stream beds with an abundance of water, and a fountain would flow from the Temple into the Wadi Shittim—possibly the Kidron Valley to the east of the Temple mount.

34D Ruth tells how Elimelech's family line was preserved and how his Moabite daughter-in-law, Ruth, was joined in marriage to Boaz, a kinsman of Elimelech. Ruth gave birth to Obed, who was the father of Jesse, who was the father of David. That Ruth provides information about David's family tree assured it of a place in the Hebrew scriptures. Furthermore, although Ruth was a Moabitess, she gave up her country and her gods to embrace in faith the God of Israel.

34E Jonah tells how a nationalistic Jew preached with considerable reluctance to the Assyrian city of Nineveh, urging its inhabitants to repent. To Jonah's great disappointment, the city repented. He is later rebuked for caring more about the loss of a shade tree than the people of Nineveh whom God created and loves. The narrative urges postexilic Jews to adopt a more merciful attitude toward the Gentiles.

34F The stage for the narrative that unfolds in the book of Esther is Persia. The key players are two Jews who continue to reside in Persia: Esther and her older cousin Mordecai. Esther tells how the Jews were able to turn the tables on the Gentiles (led by the hated Haman the Agagite) who sought their destruction. The events described gave rise to the observance of the feast of Purim—a feast in which God empowered the Jews to resist and destroy their enemies. Still today, Jews who celebrate the feast of Purim are told that they may drink wine to the point where the difference between "Blessed be Mordecai" and "Cursed be Haman" becomes blurred and indistinguishable.

CROSS WAYS

4
SECTION

UNITS 31–40

The Postexilic Period and Judaism

UNIT 35
Psalms

The Psalms in the Life of Ancient Israel

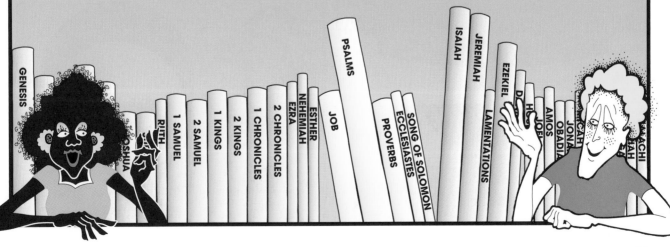

35A

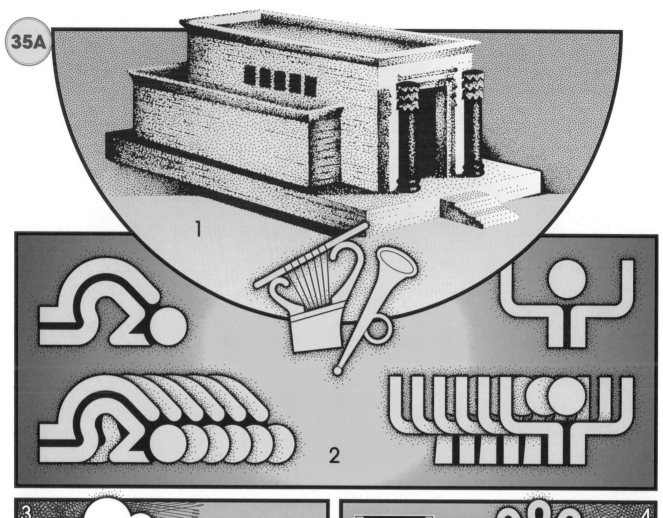

1

2

3

4

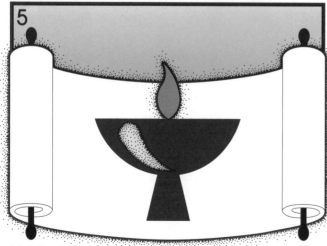

5

6

The Hebrew title for the book of Psalms is *Tehillim*, which means "Praises." The term *Psalms* is derived from the Greek word *psalmoi*, which means "songs." *Psalter* is derived from the Greek word *psalterion*, which means "a stringed instrument." The Psalms continue to play an important role in the prayer and worship life of the Jewish people. They are also used in Christian churches around the world.

The ancient Israelites believed that God had created and chosen them as His special people, rescued them in the mighty events of the Exodus from Egypt, entered into a covenant relationship with them at Sinai, led them through the wilderness to the Promised Land, and that God conquered it for them and gave it to them. They also believed that God raised up David as the nation's king. Indeed, God was involved in all that had happened to Israel—yes, even in relation to its exile in Babylon. God acted through that tragic event to discipline and renew Israel so that it might be a source of blessing and healing to surrounding nations.

Israel remembered these events and wrote them down. The people spoke with the God who orchestrated these events. They praised God. They questioned God. They reminded God of their agonies. They conversed with God as a child with a father. The Psalms echo these conversations and give insights into their historical settings.

ILLUSTRATION 35A depicts the contents of the Psalms, and the settings in which they were used.

1 The Jerusalem Temple

Temple, harp, trumpet: The Jerusalem Temple played a central role in the life of ancient Israel, particularly during the postexilic period. A variety of instruments were used in worship rituals, including harps and trumpets.

2 Laments and Songs of Praise

- **Individual Lament** (*top left*): An *individual* laments, and seeks God's help to deal with a difficulty. Approximately one-third of the Psalms fall into this category.
- **Community Lament** (*lower left*): The *community* laments a difficulty.
- **Individual Praise** (*top right*): An *individual* praises and thanks God.
- **Community Praise** (*lower left*): The *community* praises God.

3 Creation Hymns and Hymns of Historical Praise

- **Creation Hymns** (***cloud***, *top left*): The people praise God for creating and sustaining the universe.
- **Hymns of Historical Praise** (***time-line protruding from cloud; Egyptian pyramid; symbols for Mount Sinai, Sinai covenant, and God's presence at Sinai's summit***): The people praise God for involving Himself in human history—in particular, for creating the nation of Israel, for rescuing the Israelites from bondage in Egypt, for making a covenant with them at Mount Sinai.

4 Songs of Zion

- ***Jerusalem skyline:*** The people praise God for declaring Jerusalem to be His most beloved city on Planet Earth. These Psalms are sometimes referred to as "Songs of Zion."
- ***Jerusalem Temple:*** Not only does God love Jerusalem, but He dwells in the ***Holy of Holies*** in the Temple located within the city's walls. Prior to the destruction of Jerusalem and the Temple by the Babylonians in 587 B.C., the ***Ark of the Covenant*** was thought of as God's throne. ***Two winged cherubim*** stood beside the Ark, with their wings touching above it.

- **Crown:** Although God was understood to be King of creation, of all nations, and of Israel in particular, the ancient Israelites believed that God loved King David above all others, and used David and his descendants to govern the affairs of God's "chosen people."

5 Old Testament Scriptures and Wisdom

- **Scroll:** The *Old Testament scriptures*—in particular, its first five books—were (and are) held in the highest esteem by the Jewish people. During the latter part of the intertestamental period, Jewish teachers (rabbis) taught that these books were the first thing God created. God kept their contents within His mind, and eventually dictated them to Moses at Mt. Sinai. Moses produced them in written form.

- **Lamp with flame:** The rabbis equated the Pentateuch with *wisdom*, and taught that wisdom was the guiding force in the creation process. Furthermore, to know and obey God's commandments was to possess and reflect divine wisdom.

6 Sickness and Death

- **The serpent around a staff** is based on Numbers 21:1–9 and serves as a symbol for healing. Many Psalms contain references to people pleading with God to grant them help and healing in times of sickness.

- The **tombstone**, with a **skull** superimposed, serves as a symbol for death. Many ancient Israelites feared death, had little hope with regard to what awaited them after death, and begged God to lengthen their days on earth.

PSALMS—FIVE BOOKS

The Psalter is made up of collections, or books, of Psalms—five in all. Each section concludes with a doxology. This five-book structure is most likely patterned after the five books of the Pentateuch. Psalm 1 serves as an introduction, and Psalm 150 as a concluding doxology to the complete collection. The five books are:

INTRODUCTION....... Psalm 1
Book 1 .... Psalms 2–41
Book 2 .... Psalms 42–72
Book 3 .... Psalms 73–89
Book 4 .... Psalms 90–106
Book 5 .... Psalms 107–149
CONCLUSION .... Psalm 150

Classification of the Psalms

Individual Lament

 Nearly one-third of all Psalms are *Individual Laments*—prayers composed for use by individuals who came to the Temple to ask for relief from suffering, for protection against danger, or for help with guilt. The following reveals the structure and content of one of these psalms, Psalm 13.

ELEMENT	VERSE

#1 *Invocation* ....1a (O LORD)

#2 *Lament*...1–2
    a. " I "
    b. "they"
    c. "Thou"

#3 *Confession of Confidence*

#4 *Petition*... 3–4
    a. hear! turn!
    b. intervene!
    c. vs. enemies
    (Oracle-Response)

#5 *Praise/Vow to Praise* 5–6

Not all Individual Laments contain all the elements of the liturgical actions. Psalm 13, for example, lacks element #3. There is often a remarkable change in mood from dire lament to praise, e.g., vv. 5,6. How are we to account for this? Some believe that, in the interval between the final parts of the Psalm, a priest spoke words of assurance, stating that God had heard the suppliant's prayer and would grant deliverance, to which the worshiper responded with a vow of praise.

In #1, the psalmist sets out to establish contact with God. He says he feels cut off from God and wants to make sure that God is listening. The problem outlined in #2 is usually one or more of the following:

- The person is desperately sick, even at the point of death.
- Enemies are accusing him of crimes (falsely).
- Legal penalties hang over his head.

In the midst of these troubles, the psalmist suggests that God should hear him and grant his petition for any of the following reasons:

    a. It is God's nature to act that way.
    b. God is just and punishes injustice.
    c. God must be true to His covenant promises.
    d. God has acted with compassion in the past.
    e. By acting, God will demonstrate His glory before Israel and the Gentiles.
    f. It is to God's advantage to keep the worshiper alive.
    g. The psalmist's own faithfulness, innocence, or misery should move God to action.

Community Lament

1 These are collective or national petitions in which the community as a whole is suffering an affliction such as a drought or a reversal in war. Generally, they contain the same elements as the **Individual Lament**, although element #3 is usually a *Review of God's Past Help*, rather than a *Confession of Confidence*.

2 Psalm 80 is an example of a Community Lament:
#1, vv. 1–3; #2, vv. 4–7,12f; #3, vv. 8–11; #4, vv. 14–17; #5, v. 18. A refrain occurs at vv. 3,7,19.

Individual Narrative Praise and Community Narrative Praise

These Psalms of praise will be considered together. They were apparently intended to accompany an offering made in gratitude for some benefit received. They declare God's goodness, greatness, and faithfulness to the covenant. Their usual elements are:

Individual Praise (Psalm 30)	**Community Praise** (Psalm 124)
#1 *Introduction* 1–3	#1 *Introduction* 1–5
a. Summons	a. Summons
b. Initial summary	b. Initial summary
c. Crisis in retrospect	
#2 *Call to Praise* ....4–5 "Praise! Blessed!"	#2 *Call to Praise* 6a
#3 *Account (Narrative)* 6–12a	#3 *Account of God's Deed* 6b–7
a. Crisis in retrospect 6–7	
b. Rescue 8–12	
● "I pleaded" 8–10	
● "You intervened" 11–12a	
#4 *Close: Praise/Vow to Praise* 12b	#4 *Close: Expression of Confidence* 8

Descriptive Praise (Hymns)

The basic structure that underlies these psalms is illustrated in Psalm 113:

#1 *Call to Praise* 1–3

#2 *Twofold Reason: God's Attributes* 4–9
   a. The LORD is great (Majesty)...........................4–6
   b. The LORD is good (Compassion)...............7–9a
     ● The LORD saves
     ● The LORD preserves.

#3 *Close: Hallelujah!*...9b

Not all Psalms of a specific category follow precisely the structure of the examples listed above. Elements of the basic structure are missing in some. Variant types occur. To illustrate:

Individual Lament
Sometimes one characteristic of a Psalm type is picked up and developed into a Psalm itself. Psalm 23 can be classified as a **Psalm of Trust**, or a **Psalm of Confidence**. It reflects #3 of the basic pattern of this Psalm type. Psalm 51, one of the best-known of the individual laments, can also be classified as a **Psalm of Repentance**. It picks up #2 of this Psalm type.

Psalm of Descriptive Praise
Several variations occur.

- **Creation Psalms** proclaim God's greatness as Creator. In these, #2a has become an independent Psalm, e.g., 8, 29, 104.
- **History Psalms** combine element #2 of **Community Narrative Praise** (*Call to Praise*) with element #2a of **Psalms of Descriptive Praise** to point to God's greatness and actions as the Lord of History, e.g., Psalm 78.
- In a third variation, a **Liturgical Imperative** appears between the two statements about God being "great" (#2a) and God being "good" (#2b). It begins with either a direct command, "Praise! Come!" or an exhortation, "Let us come!" e.g., Psalm 95.

Community Narrative Praise
- Two variations within this group are known as **Victory Songs** (e.g., Judges 5) and **Epiphany Psalms**, e.g., Psalms 18:7–15; 29.

Liturgies

The Psalter contains a variety of psalms that have been shaped by specific liturgical needs and acts.

1 **Pilgrimage Psalms** and **Songs of Zion:** The Psalter contains only one pilgrim song, Psalm 122. There are allusions to them elsewhere, Isaiah 2; Jeremiah 31:6. The Psalter does contain a number of Songs of Zion that are closely related in spirit to Psalm 122. These songs glorify Jerusalem and God's plans for it, Psalms 46, 76, 84, 87. Psalm 122 concentrates on the *actual journey to the Holy City*, which was seen to be virtually a sacred ritual.

2 **Entrance Liturgies:** In ancient pagan temples, worshipers inquired about the rites to be performed, and the ritual purity to be observed, at the sanctuary they were approaching. Priests replied by explaining the requirements for entering the presence of their particular deity.

In Israel, this was adapted so that a kind of *moral catechizing* took place. The conditions for approaching and worshiping God in the Jerusalem Temple were of a moral order: purity, justice, loyalty to the Sinai covenant. It was the priests' duty to expound this to the Israelites as they approached for worship. Their right to approach was based on the mercy of God promised and given in the covenant. The worshipers' statements declared that they wished to take the covenant relationship seriously. Psalm 15 is an example of an entrance liturgy. Verse 1 of this psalm poses the question of *worthiness of approach*. The verses that follow answer the question.

3 **Procession with the Ark of the Covenant:** Psalm 24 is an example of such a Psalm. It consists of a brief hymn (vv. 1,2) and two liturgical dialogues (vv. 3–6,7–10). Apparently this Psalm was sung in a procession carrying the Ark of the Covenant back into the Temple after it had been carried out to battle, or for some other purpose. The opening hymn speaks of God as the creator of the world. The first dialogue is similar to Psalm 15; it stresses the moral requirements for entering the Lord's Temple.

Enthronement Psalms

In these Psalms, God is greeted as King. This was not to suggest that God had not always been King. God had indeed! But this truth is now celebrated. God sits enthroned over all creation. God is King because of His creative power (93:1–4; 95:3–5; 98:7,8) and because of the Exodus event in which He saved Israel. God is King, not only over Israel, but over the whole earth; all are summoned to praise the God who is "above all gods." These Psalms look forward to the time when the God of Israel will rule over all nations. Psalms 47, 93, 95–100 are usually classified as Enthronement Psalms.

Royal Psalms

Psalms 2, 18, 20, 21, 45, 72, 89, 101, 110, and 132 focus on events relating to the experiences of the king:

- Accession to the throne, 2, 72, 110
- Marriage, 45
- Thanksgiving for victory in war, 18, 21
- Prayers for the safety and victory of the king, 20
- Directions for how the king is to rule, 101
- A royal lament, 89
- Psalm 132 links a promise on behalf of Zion with one on behalf of the Davidic dynasty, both of whom were divinely chosen.

It is significant that Royal Psalms were preserved and used after the exile—a period devoid of kings. Possibly, they were preserved because the community heard in them the announcement of better days and hope for the future. Most likely the Davidic dynasty had played too prominent a role in the life of Israel for these psalms to disappear.

Wisdom Psalms

These Psalms deal with issues such as the problem of retribution, the difference between the just and the unjust, and the blessings conferred by wisdom. They contain a didactic or teaching tone, beatitudes ("Blessed are…"), and are sometimes acrostic in structure. In acrostic Psalms (e.g., Psalm 119), successive verses, or groups of verses, begin with the twenty-two successive letters of the Hebrew alphabet.

The following are usually classified as Wisdom Psalms: 1; 36:1–4; 37; 49; 73; 112; 127; 128; 133. The Psalms that praise the **Law** also belong to this group, 19:7–14; 119.

1 There are many references in the Psalms to the Temple and the sacrificial system. For the Israelite, God dwelt in the Temple where worshipers made contact with Him through song and offerings. The whole range of human feelings toward God is found in the Psalms, including praise, thanksgiving, lament, and complaint.

2 A sense of community prevails throughout the Psalms. Even when the psalmist's prayer has a personal tone, he either invites others to praise the Lord with him, or he shares the lesson of his experience with others.

3 The Psalms refer constantly to two truths about the Lord. God is both *Creator* and *Savior*. As *Creator*, God sits enthroned above creation and rules it with providential care on behalf of His people. The events of the Exodus are mentioned frequently in references to God as *Savior*. These allusions either summon the people to praise, or make their unfaithfulness all the more incomprehensible, 78; 136:10–22.

4 The Psalms insist that God's character is constant. Those who yearn for forgiveness, or are threatened by death or the plots of their enemies, can approach God with childlike trust. The psalmist could ask, "Lord, where is Your steadfast love of old?" 89:49. God is constantly ready to hear and deliver.

5 The act of worship places moral obligations on the worshiper. This is evident from the **Entrance Liturgies**, and from Psalms 19 and 119 which speak of the Law as God's precious gift to Israel.

6 The note of joy appears repeatedly in Psalms of praise and thanksgiving. Worshipers declare their joy in God with song and dance, with shouts and gestures, with wonder and delight. They bear witness to God and proclaim His wondrous deeds with gratitude and enthusiasm.

7 Two features present difficulties to the modern Christian reader of the Psalms.

    a. Some of the Psalms contain violent denunciations of enemies, and pray for vengeance on them. The classic example of this is 137:7–9, which can in no way be reconciled with the command to love one's enemies. However, those who suffered because of their allegiance to God thought of their enemies as God's enemies also. The psalmist sees the wicked as opposed to God and therefore as deserving of punishment. The wicked are often described in a stylized way, as are the punishments suggested for them.

    b. Many passages in the Psalms deny the worth of any existence after death. Death meant separation from the Lord. It meant entry into a shadowy and joyless existence in a murky underworld called Sheol. How much reason there was, then, to love this present life with all its God-given blessings! In Sheol, all was gone. As Psalm 6:5 expresses it, "For in death there is no remembrance of You; in Sheol who can give You praise?" Even so, there are passages in Psalms that seem to rise above the belief that this earthly life is all there is to existence, 16:9–11; 49:13–15; 73:21–26. In these, the psalmist declares his conviction that the fellowship he enjoys with God in this present life outweighs the afflictions he has to endure; it is a possession which even death cannot take away.

8 A puzzling issue is the fact that the authorship of many Psalms is attributed to David. In some of the Psalms attributed to him, the writer makes reference to worshiping God in the Jerusalem Temple (Psalm 5:7) which *was built only after David's death*. He also fears the approach of death, and embraces no hope of life after death, Psalm 30:8–10.

Although the psalms were written over a long period of time, they were only included in the Hebrew Scriptures during the period A.D. 70–100 (as part of *The Writings*). Superscriptions denoting authorship were added long after the Psalms were written. It is possible that the people of Judah ascribed numerous psalms to David simply because they held him in great esteem.

SUMMARY

The Book of Psalms served ancient Israel as its prayer, liturgy, and hymn book. It was used in particular by the postexilic community, although many psalms were composed and used before the Babylonian exile.

The Psalter contains numerous Psalm types: laments by both individual and community; hymns of different kinds; pilgrimage Psalms; entrance liturgies; and Psalms that praise God for God's acts in both creation and redemption. Some deal with the life of the royal family. Others celebrate the Kingship of God over creation. Some sing the praises of the Law and God's gift of wisdom.

Psalm Types

It is virtually impossible to summarize the Book of Psalms. The Bible student should be familiar with at least one typical example of the main classifications dealt with in this unit. The following summary of Psalm types is also helpful:

PSALM	LAMENT	PRAISE	PRAISE (HYMN)	ENTHRONE-MENT •ROYAL	WISDOM *LITURGY
1					Law
2				•Royal	
3	Individual				
4	Individual				
5	Individual Innocence				
6	Individual				
7	Individual Innocence				
8			Creation		
9		Individual			
10	Individual				
11	Individual				
12	Individual				
13	Individual				
14			Composite (=53)		
15					*Entrance
16	Individual				
17	Individual Innocence				
18		Individual Thanksgiving		•Royal	
19			Creation		Law

PSALM	LAMENT	PRAISE	PRAISE (HYMN)	ENTHRONE-MENT •ROYAL	WISDOM *LITURGY
20				•Royal	
21				•Royal	
22	Individual				
23	Individual Confidence				
24					*Entrance *Ark
25	Individual				
26	Individual Innocence				
27	Individual				
28	Individual				
29		Community Epiphany	Imperative Creation	Enthrone-ment	
30		Individual			
31	Individual				
32		Individual			
33			Descriptive		
34		Individual			
35	Individual				
36	Individual				
37					Wisdom
38	Individual				
39	Individual				

62

PSALM	LAMENT	PRAISE	PRAISE (HYMN)	ENTHRONEMENT •ROYAL	WISDOM *LITURGY
40	Individual	Individual			
41		Individual		Composite	
42	Individual				
43	Individual				
44	Community				
45				•Royal	
46					*Zion
47				Enthrone-ment	
48					*Zion
49					Wisdom
50			Miscellaneous		
51	Individual Repentance				
52	Individual				
53			Composite (=14)		
54	Individual				
55	Individual				
56	Individual				
57	Individual				
58	Individual				
59	Individual				
60	Community				
61	Individual				
62	Individual				
63	Individual				
64	Individual				
65			Descriptive		
66	Individual	Community	Descriptive		
67					*Blessing
68			Composite		
69	Individual				
70	Individual				
71	Individual				
72				•Royal	
73	Individual				
74	Community				
75			Thanks-giving		
76					*Zion
77	Individual				
78			Historical		
79	Community				
80	Community				
81			Miscellaneous		
82			Miscellaneous		
83	Community				
84					*Zion
85	Community				
86	Individual				
87					*Zion
88	Individual				
89	Community			•Royal	
90	Community				
91			Composite		*Blessing
92		Individual			
93				Enthrone-ment	
94	Individual				Wisdom Law
95			Imperative		

PSALM	LAMENT	PRAISE	PRAISE (HYMN)	ENTHRONE-MENT •ROYAL	WISDOM *LITURGY
96				Enthrone-ment	
97				Enthrone-ment	
98				Enthrone-ment	
99				Enthrone-ment	
100			Imperative		
101				•Royal	
102	Individual				
103			Descriptive		
104			Creation		
105			Historical		
106	Individual Community		Imperative		*Blessing
107			Descriptive		
108			Composite (57 + 60)		
109	Individual				
110				•Royal	
111			Descriptive		
112					Wisdom
113					
114			Miscellaneous		
115					*Liturgy
116		Individual			
117			Imperative		
118					*Liturgy
119					Law
120			Composite		
121					*Liturgy
122					*Pilgrim-age

PSALM	LAMENT	PRAISE	PRAISE (HYMN)	ENTHRONE-MENT •ROYAL	WISDOM *LITURGY
123	Individual Confidence				
124		Community			
125	Individual Confidence				
126			Composite		
127					Wisdom
128					Wisdom
129		Community			
130	Individual				
131	Individual Confidence				
132				•Royal	*Zion
133					Wisdom
134			Imperative		
135			Descriptive		
136			Descriptive		
137			Miscellaneous		
138		Individual			
139			Creation		
140	Individual				
141	Individual				
142	Individual				
143	Individual				
144				•Royal	
145			Descriptive		
146			Descriptive		
147			Descriptive		
148			Imperative		
149			Descriptive		
150			Imperative		

CROSS WAYS®

4 SECTION

UNITS 31–40

The Postexilic Period and Judaism

UNIT 36
Wisdom Literature

The Old Testament Wisdom Literature and Its Themes

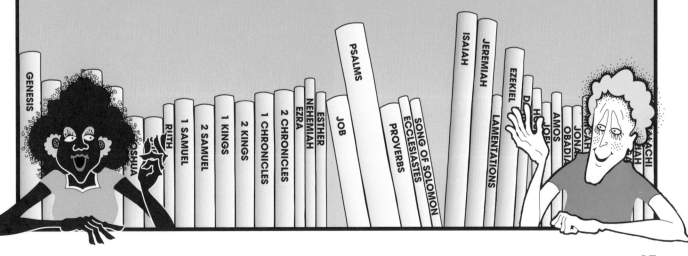

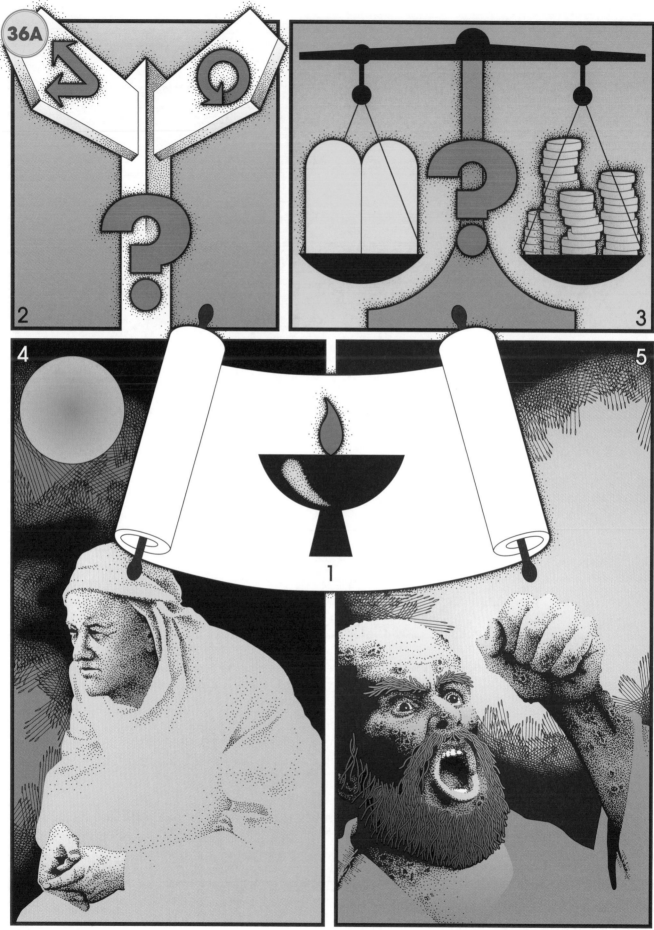

Wisdom Literature

ILLUSTRATION 36A depicts the concept of wisdom as it was understood and practiced within ancient Israel.

Concepts

Lamp, flame (symbol for wisdom), *center:* The ancient Israelites believed that there is a final truth, a final wisdom, in the universe that humanity should seek to know and believe, and to which it should conform. Those who know, believe, and conform to it are in harmony with God, creation, others, and themselves. *They possess wisdom!*

Open scroll: Toward the close of the Old Testament era, some rabbis equated wisdom with the Old Testament scriptures, but more specifically with the Pentateuch (Genesis through Deuteronomy). The Old Testament contains a number of wisdom writings: Job, Proverbs, Ecclesiastes, some of the Psalms, and—according to some—The Song of Solomon. These writings advise a person how to experience the greatest meaning and satisfaction in life.

Signpost and question mark, *top left:* The wisdom writings teach that every person walks in either *the way of the righteous* (symbol for obedience, *left*), or *the way of the wicked* (symbol for disobedience, *right*).

Scales, question mark, commandments, coins, *top right:* The wisdom writings ask questions about the relationship between obedience and material prosperity.

Ecclesiastes

Person looking glum under the sun, *lower left:* The writer of Ecclesiastes rejected the idea that the study of wisdom could enable people to discover the divine plan behind the universe. He felt that much of life is vanity and a striving after wind. There is nothing new under the sun!

Job

Person with angry face and sores on body, *lower right:* Job probes questions in relation to motives for actions and reasons for suffering in life. Do the righteous obey God because of the blessings that might accrue as a result? How are the righteous to understand their relationship with God when the burdens they encounter in life become unbearable?

Old Testament wisdom literature makes little reference to the exodus from Egypt, election, covenant and law-codes, the Day of the Lord, the Jerusalem Temple, the priesthood, messianic hopes, and great personalities and events. Its concern is to probe the meaning of life, and to give practical advice about how to attain and enjoy the successful and good life.

Solomon and Wisdom

1 First Kings reports that God appeared to Solomon in a dream and said, "Ask what I should give you." Solomon replied, "Give your servant an understanding mind to govern your people, able to discern between good and evil; for who can govern this your great people?" (3:5,9). First Kings 4:29–34 states that God *gave* wisdom to Solomon. Just as God gave His instructions to the priests and His word to the prophets, so, too, God gave wisdom to the wise.

The next verse indicates that, although other wise men lived at the time of Solomon, they were less endowed with wisdom than was Solomon. According to Old Testament writings, Solomon gave concrete expression to his wisdom in the way he handled disputes and ruled his realm. While 1 Kings 10 concentrates on material aspects of Solomon's reign, 1 Kings 11 states that Solomon was not as wise as some thought him to be. He built altars for the worship of foreign gods, and himself worshiped those gods.

2 The Old Testament ascribes *Proverbs* and *Ecclesiastes* to Solomon. The opening verse of *Song of Solomon* ascribes this work to Solomon also, possibly because 1 Kings 4:32 says he composed many proverbs and songs. However, it is doubtful that Solomon produced this collection of love songs in which a man and a woman speak of their attraction for each other. They were accepted into the Old Testament canon only because they were reinterpreted as allegories depicting the love of God for Israel. Non-canonical writings are also ascribed to Solomon: *The Wisdom of Solomon*, *The Psalms of Solomon*, and *The Odes of Solomon*.

Solomon's wisdom was said to surpass that of "all the people of the east" and that "of Egypt." Solomon's reputation for wisdom persuaded the queen of Sheba to visit him to hear it for herself. She *heard* it, for he was able to answer all of her questions, 1 Kings 10:3. She *saw* its fruits demonstrated in the magnificence of Solomon's court until "there was no more spirit in her," 1 Kings 10:5.

1 The children of Israel once lived in Egypt. Solomon was married to an Egyptian princess, 1 Kings 3:1. Deuteronomy 17:14–17 hints at a continuing contact between the two realms during the time of Solomon. Egypt had wisdom writings known as *Sebayit* written to serve as teaching materials to train and equip rulers and officials. Some Old Testament wisdom literature resembles these writings, which often reflect the spirit and style of a father talking to a son. There are also obvious similarities in content between Jewish and other Egyptian wisdom writings—for example, Proverbs 22:17–24:22 and the *Instruction of Amen-em-ope*.

2 Wisdom literature from Mesopotamia concerned itself more with magic and cultic practices. Some parallels do exist. *The Counsels of Wisdom* are similar in tone and content to Proverbs. They consist of moral exhortations that appear to be the admonitions of a ruler to his son. They use the phrase "my son" frequently, and the subjects they deal with resemble those of Proverbs.

3 Israel's wisdom materials are unique for they were shaped by the conviction that Israel was a nation under the Lord. They speak to *all within the nation*, not just to those at the royal court. The training of leaders and officials gave way to the training of every Israelite. The "son" or "student" of Proverbs and Sirach is every Jew, Deuteronomy 4:6. The subjects dealt with in the biblical wisdom literature are broader in scope. Although they refer to trees, hyssop, beasts, birds, reptiles, and fish, their prime concern is life under God.

1 The Book of Proverbs is a "collection of collections" of teaching materials, originally designed for use by professional teachers in the instruction of youth.

    chs. 1–9 .... The value of wisdom
    10:1–22:16 .... The proverbs of Solomon
    22:17–24:22 .... The words of the Wise
    24:23–24 .... Sayings of the Wise
    chs. 25–29 .... The proverbs of Solomon collected by the men of King Hezekiah
    ch. 30 .... The words of Agur, the son of Jakeh
    31:1–9 .... The words of Lemuel, king of Massa
    31:10–31 .... A poem about the good housewife

2 Each proverb is a poetic two-line saying, usually crisp and short, that deals with some aspect of human experience. The most obvious characteristic of Hebrew poetry is *parallelism*—each sentence usually has two parts to it. In what is known as *synonymous parallelism*, the second line repeats the idea expressed in the first line, with a slight variation:

> *Drive out a scoffer, and strife goes out;*
>   *and quarreling and abuse will cease.* (Prov. 22:10)

3 Sometimes the two lines say the same thing by way of *negation* or *contrast*. This is known as *antithetic parallelism*:

> *A wise child makes a glad father,*
>   *but a foolish child is a mother's grief.* (Prov. 10:1)

4 In the *staircase* or *ascending parallelism*, the second line completes the thought of the first:

> *Like a gold ring in a pig's snout*
>   *is a beautiful woman without good sense.* (Prov. 11:22)

A sensitivity to the parallelism of Hebrew poetry can aid interpretation when the meaning of one of the lines is obscure.

5 The insights offered in Proverbs deal with the following subjects:

    a. They speak of a person's relationship with God. "The fear of the Lord is the beginning of knowledge," or a similar thought, is stated, 1:7,29; 2:5; 3:7; 8:13; 9:10 and 16:6. A summons to "trust God" occurs at 3:5,23–26; 16:20; 18:10. These terms complement one another. Both refer to what should be the deepest concern in any person's life: one's relationship to God. God's actions and will are to set the boundaries for all human plans, 10:22; 16:33; 19:21; 20:24. The desired outcome is that the wise might be equipped to understand the meaning of life. The fool, no matter how clever he may appear on the surface, will always grope in confusion.

    b. Proverbs speaks about the Two Ways: the way of the wise and the foolish; the way of the righteous and the wicked. Behind its maxims lies the Deuteronomic doctrine of rewards and punishments, of blessing and curse (Deut. 28:1–14, 15–68). The righteous will flourish, 11:28; 14:11. The wicked will be overthrown and destroyed, 10:9; 11:5. However, there is a variation. An older view said that the practice of wisdom bestowed *material* success. This gave way to the view that wisdom for its own sake is the highest good in life. However, it was said that the gift of wisdom is bestowed on *good people*. Later, other explanations for life's meaning would be sought.

c. Proverbs praises wisdom repeatedly. It is a gift from God (2:6) and is the "first fruits" of God's creation, 8:22–31. From it flow real life and good fortune, 13:13; 19:8. Prudence is a fruit of wisdom. It is the demeanor that the wise exhibit at all times as they exercise moderation and self-control, 14:17; 16:32. On the other hand, folly is not merely stupidity; it is an attitude toward life, 15:2, 16:22. It demonstrates itself in thoughtlessness, excessive talk, and lack of self-control, 17:24; 19:2; 25:28. Arrogance is an abomination to the Lord, 16:5. The reader is constantly exhorted to seek and cultivate wisdom. To do this is of the utmost importance.

d. Proverbs encourages conscientious work and ridicules those who are lazy. It encourages the simple, uncluttered life and discourages seeking illicit gain. The wise should be ready to share their possessions with the needy, 14:21b, 31.

e. Proverbs offers much advice about life in the family circle, especially about bringing up children. After all, children's behavior can have considerable effect on the eventual well-being and happiness of parents, 10:1; 13:1; 15:20; 29:15–17. People are to live together harmoniously if peace is to prevail in the community. Cantankerous women are denounced repeatedly, 11:22; 17:1; 19:13; 21:9,19; 25:24; 27:15,16. On the other hand, the good wife is the most precious of jewels, 31:10–31. Advice is offered to men, husbands, and fathers, 3:30–33; 5:20–23; 6:12–15; 6:16–19. Young people are reminded of their obligation to honor the aged, 13:1, 19:26; 20:20, 23:22. Proper behavior around a meal table is important, 23:1–8.

f. The book contains many observations about the world and life within it and speaks to all within the nation, from king to slave. God's people are to be aware of the power of words to hurt and heal, and are to focus on the need to behave well, to do good, and to strive for peace.

1 Proverbs is a collection of *collections of wisdom statements* produced over a considerable span of years. Ecclesiastes, on the other hand, is the work of one person who wrote approximately 250–200 B.C. It contains statements that constituted a threat to orthodox Judaism. Some perceive evidence of touching up by orthodox editors to make the work more palatable to Jewish tastes, 2:26; 3:17; 5:19; 7:18b,26b; 8:11–13; 11:9b; 12:1a.

2 According to earlier Jewish sages, wisdom could show the right course of action and help a person understand the divine plan underlying creation. Ecclesiastes threw out a bold challenge to that position. It insisted that "all is vanity" (1:2), that a person's efforts to achieve anything amount to nothing, for character and accomplishments make no difference to a person's lot in life or fate after death (which is the same as that of the beasts!). Humanity cannot change the situation. God's wisdom is inscrutable. From the human perspective, there seems to be no reason for life. Everything appears to be a matter of chance. If there is a divine plan, humanity is left in the dark about it. History is a matter of caprice, without meaning or purpose, and moves in pointless circles. Therefore, the best thing to do is to enjoy whatever good gifts and opportunities God grants before the aging process takes its toll and death plunges one into oblivion, 11:9–12:8.

3 It is not known who wrote Ecclesiastes. The suggestion that Solomon wrote it (1:12,13; 2:4–11) is not convincing. However, the references to Solomonic authorship, plus the orthodox "improvements" mentioned above, gained it a place in the Old Testament canon. The rabbis seriously questioned the right of Ecclesiastes, Esther, and The Song of Solomon to a place in the Old Testament for several centuries, even after they were officially accepted into it. In 1:1, the writer refers to himself as "the Teacher"; the Hebrew term is *Qoheleth*, a word describing a function—one who speaks to a congregation.

4 The theme is declared in 1:2 and repeated in 12:8, "Vanity of vanities, says the Teacher... All is vanity." Qoheleth also shows a fondness for the phrase, "All is vanity and a chasing after wind," 2:17,26. He does not dismiss the value of wisdom completely. It does have some worth, for it makes a person aware of the limitations of life. Wisdom gives the wise a strength greater than ten rulers in a city. Even so, in the long run the advantages of wisdom are doubtful, for it brings an increase in vexation and sorrow (1:18), and death overtakes both the wise and the foolish. Qoheleth's advice is to enjoy life while it lasts and to make the best of it, but do not try to probe or prove the future, 2:24,25; 3:12–15; 7:14.

5 There are moments of opportunity, 3:2–9. One should try to make the best use of each moment as it comes and exercise moderation in the practice of both wisdom and folly, for to go to one extreme or the other can lead to disaster. Accordingly, a man should enjoy life with his wife and find whatever satisfaction he can in his daily work, "for there is no work, or thought, or knowledge, or wisdom in

Sheol, to which you are going," 9:9,10. Unfortunately, "the days of darkness will be many," 11:8. Life in Sheol is nothing but dust and silence.

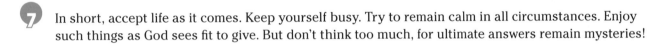

6. According to Qoheleth, the traditional Jewish attitude concerning the Two Ways did not offer a satisfactory explanation for life, or reasons for well-being, or what lay beyond death. The same fate—death!—eventually overtakes both the righteous and the unrighteous; both go to the same place, 9:1–6. Even worse, during life in this world the righteous may be anything but happy, while the unrighteous may live long and enjoy much, 7:15–18. One may work hard and accumulate much, only to die and leave it all to a loafer and a fool, 2:18–23. In some ways, it would be better not to have been born at all, 2:17; 4:1–3. Qoheleth's attitude to life is summed up in 5:18–20.

> *This is what I have seen to be good: It is fitting to eat and drink and find enjoyment in all the toil with which one toils under the sun the few days of the life God gives us; for this is our lot. Likewise all to whom God gives wealth and possessions and whom he enables to enjoy them, and to accept their lot and to find enjoyment in their toil—this is the gift of God. For they will scarcely brood over the days of their lives, because God keeps them occupied with the joy of their hearts.*

7. In short, accept life as it comes. Keep yourself busy. Try to remain calm in all circumstances. Enjoy such things as God sees fit to give. But don't think too much, for ultimate answers remain mysteries!

Song of Solomon

 It is difficult to know how to classify or interpret the Song of Solomon. English Bibles group it with Job, Proverbs, and Ecclesiastes, giving the impression that the Song is a wisdom writing. The ascription of the work to Solomon has helped support this view, 1:1. However, the ascription to Solomon is editorial only. The contents appear to be postexilic, possibly from the third century B.C., although much of the material is possibly much older. The work has been interpreted in different ways.

   a. Some interpret the Song allegorically and seek spiritual meaning in every detail. The Jewish community saw God as the lover and Israel as the beloved. The Christian community saw Jesus as the Lover and the Church as the beloved. Those who interpreted it this way thought that songs about human physical love were not worthy of a place in God's Word.

   b. Some suggest that the Song reflects worship practices in the ancient fertility cults, and speaks of nature returning to life after the harshness of winter. The allusions in the work are too vague to support this view.

   c. Others interpret the Song as love poetry depicting the moods of lovers in courtship. They experience happiness when they are together, and pain when they are apart.

 The first approach suggested has numerous supporters who insist that although the Song does not mention the name of God, God is present everywhere. They believe that the entire work must be read as a parable whose message can be understood only in the light of the poem as a whole. They appeal to several passages to support their view: Isaiah 5:1–6; 54:4–8; Jeremiah 2:2f,32; Hosea 1–3. Those who advocate the third view interpret the work to be supporting a deep rather than transient relationship, and reflecting the Old Testament's teaching on continuing creation. Genesis 1 describes God's initial creative act. Genuine love among humans perpetuates that initial act.

Job

Job is the most sublime example of wisdom writing in the Old Testament. It is difficult to determine when it was written, and who wrote it. The book makes little mention of the traditional themes of Israel's faith. The story is not set in Jerusalem, but on the edge of the desert. The central figure is not an Israelite, but an Edomite sheik from the land of Uz; see Genesis 10:23; Jeremiah 25:19ff; Lamentations 4:21; Job 1:1. Some suggest the book was written by a Jew living on the fringes of Palestine. The fact that the Edomites are referred to in a favorable light suggests that the *story about Job* was written before the kind of animosity evident in Obadiah 10–14 developed towards the Edomites. Most likely, the *poetic section* was written later; suggestions range from the preexilic period to the fifth or fourth century B.C. But knowing when Job was written offers little help for understanding the book's timeless message and application.

The Story

1 Many think that the aim of the book is to depict Job as the supreme example of how to endure suffering calmly and serenely. It is traditional to refer to the patience of Job. One can obtain this impression of Job by reading only the prologue (1:1–2:13) and the epilogue (42:7–17), and neglecting to read what comes in between. In the poetic section, Job demonstrates anything but patience, curses the day he was born, and all but shakes his fist in the face of God. Only after his fury has spent itself and God has rebuked him does he repent, and only then does his inner storm yield to an inner stillness.

2 The brief prose section tells the story of a man called Job. Job had a reputation for godliness and enjoyed all the good things that were considered divine reward for piety. However, Job's piety came under the scrutiny of "the Satan"—in this context, that member of God's Heavenly Council whose special duty was to watch closely what was happening on earth and to bring necessary matters to God's attention. Only the reader witnesses this opening debate between God and the Satan (or "the Accuser").

3 God let it be known to the Satan just how He felt about Job, 1:8. The Satan responded by suggesting that Job's piety stemmed from self-interest, and that if he were deprived of his possessions, it would be a different story altogether. The Lord then gave the Satan permission to put his theory to the test, with the proviso that Job was not to suffer any physical harm. Although Job eventually lost all his possessions, and all his family except his wife, his faith remained unshaken. He confessed, "Naked I came from my mother's womb, and naked shall I return there; the Lord gave, and the Lord has taken away; blessed be the name of the Lord," 1:21.

4 The Satan then suggested a more severe test for Job's piety—that he be afflicted with vile sores from head to toe. The Lord agreed to this second test, with the proviso that Job not be deprived of his life. Accordingly, Job was reduced to a condition in which he sat among ashes and scraped his sores with a piece of broken pottery to obtain relief from his pain and agonies. He dismissed his wife's suggestion that he "curse God and die" with the words, "Shall we receive the good at the hand of God, and not the bad?" 2:10. He then received a visit from three of his friends, Eliphaz, Bildad, and Zophar. The visitors were shocked by what they saw, expressed their grief in typical oriental fashion, and then sat with Job in silence for seven days and seven nights, 2:11–13. However, in the poetic section that follows, the tone changes.

5. In ch. 3 Job himself speaks. He curses the day of his birth, laments that he ever saw the light of day, and agonizes over his present lot in life. He would love to die, but cannot. In the dialogue that follows a careful structure is evident.

    a.   The prose prologue sets the scene (1:1–2:13).

    b.   Three cycles of dialogue between Job and his friends:

        Job laments his lot (ch. 3).

        i.   First cycle of dialogue:
            Eliphaz (chs. 4,5)
                Job's response (chs. 6,7)
            Bildad (ch. 8)
                Job's response (chs. 9,10)
            Zophar (ch. 11)
                Job's response (chs. 12–14)

        ii.   Second cycle of dialogue:
            Eliphaz (ch. 15)
                Job's response (chs. 16,17)
            Bildad (ch. 18)
                Job's response (ch. 19)
            Zophar (ch. 20)
                Job's response (ch. 21)

        iii.   Third cycle of dialogue:
            Eliphaz (ch. 22)
                Job's response (23:1–24:17,25)
            Bildad (25:1–6; 26:5–14)
                Job's response (26:1–4; 27:1–12)
            There is debate about who speaks in 24:18–24 and 27:13–23)
                Job's response gives way to a section on wisdom (ch. 28)

        Job's final defense (chs. 29–31).

    c..   The Lord answers Job from the whirlwind:

        i.   The Lord's first speech (chs. 38,39; 40:1,2)
                Job's submission (40:3–5)

        ii.   The Lord's second speech (40:6–41:34)
                Job's repentance (42:1–6)

    d.   The closing epilogue (42:7–17)

6. In the above outline, reference to chs. 32–37 is omitted. This section consists of a rebuke of Job by Elihu. This section is thought to be an addition to the original work, for Elihu is not mentioned in either the prologue or in the epilogue as one of Job's friends, has nothing to say during the other three rounds of dialogue, and what he has to say appears to be an afterthought following the statement, "The words of Job are ended," 31:40. Elihu's speech pushes the traditional Jewish line of thought more vigorously than do the speeches of the three friends.

The Issues

1. Although a popular opinion is that the purpose of the book is to explore the issue of suffering, Job probes a much deeper issue: The nature and character of a person's relationship to God. Why should a person serve God? Does anyone have a right to expect anything from God in return for service? This issue is clear already in the opening prologue where the Satan suggests to God that Job is only serving God because of what is in it for him. What follows probes *the meaning of suffering* in the life of a just person and its *consequences* in terms of that person's attitude to God.

2 Behind all this is a question that had long been discussed by Israel's sages. Israel's wisdom teachers stressed the efficacy of righteous living. In their efforts to understand human existence, they set out to analyze the arbitrary elements in life. They maintained that there are moral laws governing life of which God is the custodian and guarantor. These laws can be known, and a person can live in harmony with them. The goal of the wise, then, is to live prudently and blamelessly. To do so is to be assured of happiness and success.

3 The arguments Job's three friends put to him are based on this Deuteronomic notion. They argue that because *righteousness* is invariably rewarded with material blessings in this life, and *unrighteousness* with poverty, sickness, and an unhappy or premature death, *the reason for Job's suffering lay in himself.* All people have sinned, and Job should confess rather than shake his fist at God. Because the reason for Job's suffering lay within Job himself, the cure for his condition must also lie within himself. The friends insist that God is always just, and that God *always* operates according to the Deuteronomic view. They accuse Job of pride and suggest that it is remarkable that, although his sin is *so great*, God is punishing him *so little*.

4 Throughout the narrative, Job insists on his innocence and rejects the arguments of his accusers. He says their comments contain no comfort and offer him no help in his search for meaning in life. He admits that he might have sinned. After all, all humanity does. At the same time, he insists that he has done nothing to deserve what has overtaken him. At first he curses his lot and hopes for death. Later he explodes with unrestrained words of protest. The reason for his present misery lies with God! God is responsible for his wretched condition! If only he could meet with God for debate, he would establish his integrity, prove his innocence, and vindicate himself, 31:37. Job sets himself up as a judge of God! "Let the Almighty answer me!", 31:35.

5 Job was able to refute the attacks of his friends. But how was Job to deal with God? Where was he to find God, 23:3? Job is torn between uncertainty and hope. He feels that God would not abandon him—indeed, that God would come searching for him. However, he fears that God will find him when it is too late, when he is already in the grave, 7:21. He is so conscious of how futile it is for humanity to try to bridge the gulf between itself and God, 9:32,33. Humanity cannot know God unless He reveals His presence. There is no way humanity can reach out and draw God into fellowship with itself. Even so, Job hopes desperately that one day the great gap between God and himself will be done away with, and that he will be able to see God as He really is. How fragile earthbound humanity is! How much it is controlled by the power of sin! How helpless in the face of death! (4:17–21; 7:6; 14:1–6; 15:14–16; 25:4–6).

The Answer

Job had insisted on his innocence to the point where he was acting as though God were denying it! However, he overvalued his innocence. He used it as a bargaining point. He held it up before God and said: "For this, my innocence, You owe me happiness! Why aren't You sticking to the rules? Why do You permit me to suffer?" God finally speaks a word from heaven. God speaks to the tormented, raging, devout, rebellious Job. What God says is brilliant. He does not provide Job with an answer, but puts his whole situation into that kind of perspective in which he no longer needs one. Throughout the response, God merely puts to Job, in majestic manner, a series of unanswerable questions. God's answer goes something like this, chs. 38,39:

1 "Anyone who sets himself up as a critic of Me had better know what he is talking about. Anyone who sets out to correct Me must himself have divine knowledge."

God pretends to believe that Job has divine knowledge, and cross-examines him on the divine activity in the universe. After all, if Job is incapable of the simplest answer, how can he hope to debate with God, and how can God hope to explain to him those mysteries that have to do with God's providence over humanity and treatment of those who are dear to Him? How? In answering, God refers to the most familiar phenomena of nature: the stars, the weather, the land, the sea, and a selection of beasts and birds. Everywhere are marvels. Mystery is everywhere. Two points emerge: *first*, God's loving concern

for His countless unsophisticated creatures; *second*, the infinite variety and richness of creation, extending to beings that seem grotesque and monstrous. In the divine wisdom they have their place, and God finds pleasure in them. The analogy holds true in the moral order, where God's ways are not always humanity's ways.

2 God responds further to Job:

"Job, let's look into this problem. Just who and what are you, Job? Do you know anything about My counsel? Do you know anything about the history of creation? Were you there when it all began? Do you know your way around the universe? Do you know what the distant corners of the universe contain? Do you know how the universe functions? If you gave it orders, would it obey?

"Job, are you in a position to feed those many little creatures on the earth? Remember that even the most strong and fierce of both beasts and birds depend on Me for their food and offspring. Are you able to exercise control over the wild animals? Take, for example, the mountain goat. It needs no help in giving birth to its young, but I know the moment when any female becomes pregnant and what that will mean for it. I see to it that the wild ass gets all the pastures it needs. Then there is the wild ox! It serves *Me*, but would it serve *you*? How much do you understand about the fiery nature of the horse?"

3 By this time, Job is beginning to feel rather small, 40:1–5. Even so, God is not through with him, 40:6–41:34.

"Job, how much do you really know about divine justice? Could you administer it? Are you so convinced about your own righteousness that, in any discussion between You and me, you assume from the outset that *I am unjust*? You are wrong, Job! No such relationship can exist between the Creator and one of the Creator's creatures! Only the omnipotent, all-seeing controller of the world can lay claim to perfect justice. Beware lest your self-righteousness cause you to condemn Me! Job, look at Behemoth! Look at Leviathan! Can you play with such creatures? I can play with them as I please. Can you or anything else overcome them or gain control of them? Remember, though, that these are My creatures, that I care for them, and that I am pleased with them."

Job's repentance

1 In the opening section of the final chapter (42:1–6), Job confesses his pride. He acknowledges that God's ways are past human understanding. His faith in his own position had been strong enough to withstand the arguments of his three friends, but when he finds himself face to face with God, he crumbles. The dark night is over. It brings joy to him to renounce his presumption, his misguided speculations, and his complaints. He even discards his last support—his famous integrity. He cannot buy his vindication from God. He must take it as a gift.

2 In the closing prose section (42:7–17), God speaks with Eliphaz and declares that He is angry with him and his friends. The doctrine they set forth, the conclusions they drew from it, and the accusations that they made were false! They must offer a burnt offering in Job's presence, and Job must pray for them. They comply, and Job's intercession is effective. God treats them with mercy. Nothing is said about the removal of Job's physical suffering. However, his possessions are restored to him twofold—which is perhaps a way of saying that he is now doubly dear to God.

3 Job never questioned the idea that material goods come as a result of the goodness and love of God. What he denied was that they were always and only withdrawn from the wicked. It is not necessary to explain why God bestows good gifts. Job sought an answer to why God withdraws them. God may withdraw them from those who are *sinners*. God may also withdraw them from those who are *virtuous*! God does not have to explain why. Humanity must remain silent before God and take at face value the assurance, "We know that all things work together for good for those who love God," Romans 8:28.

As the book ends, all Job knows is that the innocent can indeed be afflicted for no apparent reason— with no guarantee that the reason will ever be disclosed.

1 Israel's wise men looked on wisdom as more than the end product of human reflection about life. Wisdom was the divine plan that lay behind the universe and directed it, Proverbs 3:19. Humanity should therefore strive to understand that divine plan and live in harmony with it. Those who could discern wisdom and harmonize their lives with it would be successful and at peace.

2 With the passing of time, Israel's sages said that wisdom is something that exists of itself and has a special status in the cosmos. They eventually personified wisdom. Proverbs 1:20–33 speaks of wisdom as a woman standing in the marketplace beckoning people to follow her. Proverbs 8 and 9 speak of wisdom as having a personality of its own, as someone who was present when God created the universe. Indeed, wisdom was the first thing God created, and after God created it, wisdom remained beside God like a master workman while God completed the creative activity, Proverbs 8:22–31. Wisdom is now virtually a person that exists of itself; see also Job 28:23–28.

3 Similar reflections occur in the Apocryphal writings. Ecclesiasticus 24 states that wisdom found rest only within the borders of Israel where it associated with the Jerusalem Temple and the Law of Moses.

4 Wisdom also came to be thought of as the intermediary that bridged the gulf between God and humanity, and between God's wisdom and humanity's wisdom. Although that gulf can be bridged only from God's side, it has been bridged by the divine wisdom God created and that now dwells among humanity.

5 In the New Testament, Paul identifies Wisdom with Jesus, 1 Corinthians 1:24,30. The opening verses of the prologue to John's Gospel (1:1–14) refer to Jesus as "logos" (Wisdom) and speak of Him both as the Creator and as the Divine Pattern that creation and humanity must reflect if cosmic harmony is to prevail.

36A Three classes of religious leaders existed in ancient Israel: priest, prophet, and wise man. Each spoke with the authority of God and had his own particular gift. The wise man studied life's meaning, and from his years of experience and the accumulated wisdom of the past, gave counsel. This counsel was put into written form and is known as the Wisdom Literature. Wisdom is not merely human insight, but the divine purpose that directs the universe. Humanity's goal is to discover that divine purpose and live in harmony with it. The wise man's special gift enabled him to interpret the meaning of life in the light of the Law and the Prophets. He sought to deal with issues and questions such as:

- The way of the righteous and the way of the wicked;
- The relationship between obedience and prosperity;
- Can we mere humans really understand the nature of true wisdom?
- Why do the righteous suffer?

36B First Kings 4:29–34 states that Solomon prayed to God for wisdom, and God granted his request. Although 1 Kings 10 focuses on the material splendor of Solomon's Jerusalem and the wisdom he manifested during his reign, 1 Kings 11 suggests that Solomon was not as wise as some thought; he built altars for the worship of pagan gods—and himself worshiped those gods and even endorsed the practice of child sacrifice.

36C The memory of their time in Egypt played an important role in the minds of the Israelites; the Egyptians had wisdom writings known as the *Sebayit* and the *Instruction of Amen-em-ope*. Although wisdom literature existed also in Mesopotamia, it focused on magic and cultic practices. However, *The Counsels of Wisdom* are similar in content and tone to Proverbs.

36D The Book of Proverbs is a "collection of collections" of teaching materials designed for use by professional teachers in the instruction of youth. Proverbs focuses on issues such as a person's relationship with God, the way of the righteous and the way of the wicked, the wonder of wisdom, the need to work productively and avoid laziness, and family life.

36E The writer of Ecclesiastes questioned the validity of some of the views of Israel's sages. He rejected the traditional view concerning the Two Ways and their respective consequences, maintaining that it did not adequately explain the realities of everyday life. He was pessimistic about humanity's ability to find answers to life's ultimate questions and suggested that "all is vanity and a chasing after wind."

36F Scholars debate how to classify and interpret the Song of Solomon. It is unlikely that Solomon wrote it. Some interpret it spiritually—with God as the Lover, and Israel as the beloved. Some see it as poetry depicting the moods and expressions of lovers courting each other.

36G The writer of Job raised his voice in protest against the Deuteronomic view that righteousness assured one of happiness and well-being. He probed the reasons humanity seeks to be obedient and insisted that the presence of suffering in a person's life was not necessarily an indication of past unrighteousness. God was under no obligation to lavish material blessings on the righteous and could, if He so desired, permit them to suffer for reasons known only to Himself.

36H The concept of wisdom developed until wisdom was envisioned as an entity in itself—and personified. Wisdom was the first thing God created, and after coming into existence, served God as an advisor in the initial and continuing creative process. Eventually wisdom was equated with the Law, and seen as the means God provided to bridge the gulf between Himself and humanity. The New Testament equates wisdom with Jesus the Messiah, and speaks of Jesus as both the Creator and the Divine Pattern that creation and humanity must reflect if cosmic harmony is to prevail.

CROSS WAYS

4
SECTION

UNITS 31–40

The Postexilic Period and Judaism

UNIT 37
The Intertestamental Period

The History of the Postexilic Community from 538–4 B.C.

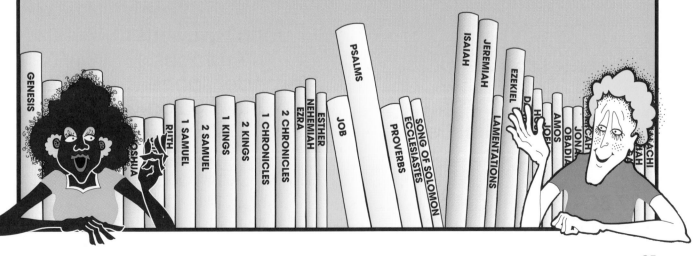

ILLUSTRATION 37A

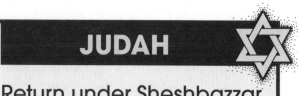

PERSIAN EMPIRE	JUDAH
538–530 Cyrus	Return under Sheshbazzar
	Altar set up
	TEMPLE rebuilding begun
530–522 Cambyses	Joshua and Zerubbabel
522–486 Darius I	TEMPLE rebuilding resumed 520
	TEMPLE dedicated 515
486–465 Xerxes I	
465–424 Artaxerxes I	Nehemiah's 2 journeys to Jerusalem
424–423 Xerxes II	
423–404 Darius II	Ezra
403–358 Artaxerxes II	
358–338 Artaxerxes III	
338–336 Arses I	
336–331 Darius III	

GREEK EMPIRE

336–323 Alexander the Great

323–198 PTOLEMIES rule Judah

198–165 SELEUCIDS rule Judah

223–187 Antiochus III	TEMPLE desecrated 168
183–175 Seleucus IV	TEMPLE rededicated 165
175–163 Antiochus IV	Judas Maccabeus 166–160
"Epiphanes"	Jonathan 160–142
	Simon 142–134
	John Hyrcanus I 134–104
	Aristobulus I 104–103

ROMAN EMPIRE

	Alexander Janneus 103–76
	Alexandra Salome 76–67
63 Pompey enters Jerusalem	Aristobulus II 67–63
44 Julius Caesar assassinated	Hyrcanus II 63–40
	Antigonus II 40–37
27 BC–14 AD Caesar Augustus	Herod the Great 37–4

ILLUSTRATION 37A provides information about the nations, rulers, and events of the postexilic period. Because the events and persons listed in the *top right corner* of this illustration are dealt with in Unit 33, no reference will be made to them in what follows. Reference to the Maccabees/Hasmoneans and Roman rulers will be made in 37B and 37C.

PERSIAN EMPIRE

1 Little is known about the history of Judah under Persian domination. The details given in Ezra and Nehemiah are limited. Information about the period is based largely on the histories of neighboring nations.

2 *Darius II* of Persia had to contend with uprisings and troubles at home and abroad. In 400 B.C., his successor, *Artaxerxes II*, lost control of Egypt—never to regain it. His unscrupulous son, *Artaxerxes III*, succeeded him.

3 To secure his position, Artaxerxes III murdered members of the royal family and other contenders for the throne. When his attempt to regain control over Egypt failed, several vassal regions revolted against Persia. After subduing one of these revolts in Sidon, Artaxerxes III managed to regain control over Egypt in 342 B.C.

4 In 338 B.C., Artaxerxes III was poisoned. He was succeeded by his son, *Arses I*, who ruled 338–336 B.C. In 336 B.C., Bagoas, the king's vizier, assassinated Arses I and placed Codomannus (known in history as *Darius III*) on the throne.

GREEK EMPIRE

1 In the year that *Darius III* ascended the throne (*336* B.C.), *Alexander the Great* came to power in Macedonia after the assassination of his father, Philip II of Macedon. Philip had ruled for twenty years, during which period he put together a military machine capable of conquering Persia.

2 Two years after taking control, Alexander crossed the Dardanelles (a narrow strait in northwestern Turkey), secured his position in western Asia, and then, in 333 B.C., headed east for battle with the Persians at Issus. Despite being outnumbered three to one, the Greeks overwhelmed the Persian forces led by Darius III. Alexander continued his advance into Egypt and then eastward into Mesopotamia until he had forged for himself a vast empire. He did not live to rule it, for he died at Babylon in *323* B.C. while returning to Greece.

3 The Jews absorbed little Persian thought or culture. They believed that they themselves possessed all religious truth in the Torah. However, things changed when the spirit of Greek Hellenism began to make its presence felt. Hellenism spoke at length about wisdom, and encouraged people to seek it like a priceless treasure. Other Hellenistic elements had to do with religion and worship, dress, games, architecture, and language. Those who assumed control after Alexander's death made earnest efforts to introduce Hellenism into all corners of the Ancient Near East, including Judah.

PTOLEMIES AND SELEUCIDS

1 After Alexander's death, his generals fought among themselves to carve up Alexander's vast empire and to increase the size of their respective realms. Between 320 and 301 B.C., southern Syria and the lands down to the borders of Egypt changed hands five times. By 312 B.C., two of the generals had established their territories as the leading powers in the Near East. *Ptolemy* ruled over Egypt, and *Seleucus* controlled what was approximately the territory of the former Babylonian Empire.

2 The High Priest of the hereditary house of Zadok (David's priest) presided at the Temple in Jerusalem, and was viewed as the leading political authority within the borders of Jewish territory.

Although during the period of Ptolemaic rule the High Priest levied taxes for the Egyptian overlords, the actual collection of those taxes was delegated to local officials recruited from leading Jewish families—one of which was the house of the Tobiads.

3 As time went by, groups of Greeks and Macedonians settled in various parts of Palestine and established communities complete with Hellenistic architectural, social, political, and religious forms. Although some Jews looked on these new innovations as an unfortunate but necessary evil, the more conservative among them bitterly resented these intrusions into their way of life. Others, such as the rich landowners, aristocracy, merchants, and officials welcomed and embraced them.

4 Seleucus, the first of the Seleucids, established his capital at Antioch on the Orontes River in Syria. One of his successors, *Antiochus III*, managed to conquer surrounding territories (including Judah) by 198 B.C. The Jewish people fared reasonably well under the new administration. The Seleucid rulers permitted them to live under their own laws, and undertook to pay for the required Temple sacrifices and to keep the Temple itself in good repair. Not only that, but the elders and Temple staff were to be exempt from taxation. Furthermore, residents in Jerusalem were granted a tax rebate for three years to encourage more people to take up residence within that city's walls. All who had been carried off from Jerusalem as slaves were to have their homes and property restored to them.

5 In 188 B.C., the Romans blocked Antiochus' international ventures. They forced him to evacuate Asia Minor, and to pay them a huge indemnity. Antiochus III died at Elam in Mesopotamia in *187* B.C., supposedly while trying to rob a temple to raise the needed money quickly. He was succeeded by his son, *Seleucus IV*, who ruled from *183* until *175* B.C.

6 The Seleucid rulers now found themselves under threat from the Egyptians to the south and the Romans to the west—with the latter seeking continually to extend their borders eastward. To complicate matters, the economic health of the realm left much to be desired. In an attempt to solve the financial problem, *Seleucus IV* tried to annul the financial privileges of those associated with the Jerusalem Temple. He also sent his chancellor, Heliodorus, to Jerusalem to extract funds from its citizens by force, 2 Maccabees 3. Eventually, Heliodorus killed Seleucus IV, and placed on the throne a younger son of Antiochus III who had been kept hostage in Rome until the indemnity demanded by the Romans in the 188 B.C. Treaty of Apamea was paid in full.

7 The new king (now released from Rome) adopted the title *Antiochus IV "Epiphanes"* (*the divine one*, "Manifestation"), believing that the Olympian god, Zeus, was manifest in him. His subjects responded by nicknaming him *"Epimanes"* (*the mad one*). Antiochus had two main goals. The first was to *unify* his realm by Hellenizing it. The second was to *expand* it. To achieve the latter he needed large sums of money.

8 To raise the needed funds, Antiochus began selling the office of High Priest in Jerusalem to the highest bidder. About 175 B.C., he deposed the incumbent High Priest, Onias III, and sold the office to Onias' pro-Hellenistic brother, Jason. Onias and many others fled to Egypt and built a temple at Leontopolis to rival that of Jerusalem.

9 Jason was deposed in 172 B.C. so that Antiochus IV could sell the office of High Priest for an even higher price to Menelaus, even though he was not a descendant of Zadok. An ardent Hellenizer, Menelaus used Temple funds to finance the purchase. When Onias III, now living in Egypt, protested, Menelaus had him murdered. When Menelaus' actions gave rise to riots and street fighting, Antiochus intervened militarily and massacred 80,000 people. Animosity developed towards Antiochus in relation to his marketing of the High-Priestly office, particularly so because Menelaus shared Antiochus' disregard for Judaism. After Jason made an unsuccessful attempt to regain office, the Syrians built a fortress (the Acra) on the hill opposite Mt. Zion and staffed it with a Syrian garrison.

10 On his return from his first campaign in Egypt (169 B.C.), Antiochus, helped by Menelaus, plundered

the Jerusalem Temple. The structure housed valuable objects used in worship, money reserved for use in the purchase of sacrificial animals, funds for the upkeep of the building itself, and private funds and property. When Antiochus carried out a second campaign into Egypt (168 B.C.), Popilius of Rome ordered him to desist immediately. Repressive measures against the Jews followed.

11 Antiochus now declared the Torah invalid. He also forbade the offering of sacrifices in the Temple, practices such as circumcision, the observance of the regular feasts, and the keeping of the Sabbath. These rites were looked on as political treason and disloyalty to Seleucid rule. The penalty for observing them was death. Eventually *the abomination of desolation*, an altar to Olympian Zeus, was set up in the Temple. Altars were also set up in other parts of the countryside and all citizens were expected to offer sacrifices at them. The choice confronting all Jews was now clear.

12 Many within Judah embraced Hellenism and supported Antiochus. Some young Jewish males had the marks of circumcision surgically reversed to be permitted to take part in athletic competitions, 1 Maccabees 1:11–15. (Those who participated in these events did so naked; women were not permitted to observe these competitions.) Athletics were linked to the honoring of Greek deities such as Heracles or Hermes, or to a ruling dynasty. In Jerusalem, the patrons of the gymnasium were foreign deities whose presence was denoted by idols.

13 The general goal of Hellenism was to establish a universal culture built on education in which all separatism was eliminated. In such a culture, Zeus could be identified with the God of Abraham, Isaac, and Jacob. The goal was not to destroy any particular state, but to fit all states into the world of Hellenism. The goal was not necessarily to *abolish* Jewish religion, but to *assimilate* it into an all-enveloping Greek culture. The High Priests appointed by Antiochus were prepared to cooperate with him in his plan to draw the Jews into the orbit of Hellenism.

14 Strong opposition to the Hellenistic movement surfaced within Judaism. The Hasidim (the *pious*, the *faithful*) were totally devoted to the observance of the Law, even to the point of refusing to take up arms to defend themselves on the Sabbath, 1 Maccabees 2:29–38. (Scholars link the origin of the Pharisees and Essenes to the Hasidim.) However, other Jews were prepared to take up arms and fight. They were more concerned with the survival of the national religion than with the strict observance of the Law.

15 The signal for battle came from a man of priestly background, Mattathias, of a family called the Hasmoneans after his great-grandfather Hasmoneus. He and his sons lived in the village of Modin northwest of Jerusalem. When an official came to Modin to demand that the people take part in pagan sacrifice, Mattathias refused to do so, and killed the official and a fellow-Jew who sacrificed as required. Mattathias then fled into the Judean wilderness, where friends and sympathizers rallied around him. The wars that followed reflected the long-standing tension between the conservative Jews living in the countryside and those living in cosmopolitan, Hellenized Jerusalem.

16 The rebels at first limited themselves to destroying pagan altars, killing apostates, and circumcising children who had been left uncircumcised. Their opponents retaliated by attacking them on the Sabbath, hoping that the rebels would continue to observe that day in good Jewish style. But when Mattathias heard of the massacre of a thousand people who had refused to take up arms on the Sabbath, he gave permission to fight the Syrian Seleucids also on that sacred day, 1 Maccabees 2:41.

17 Mattathias was killed during the first three months of fighting, and leadership of the group passed to his third son **Judas**, nicknamed **Maccabeus**, "The Hammer," because under him the rebellion developed into a full-scale war against the government forces. Although the Hasidim at first embraced the goals of Judas and his followers, they eventually withdrew their support.

Details about the Maccabean campaigns and the subsequent rule by their descendants, the Hasmoneans, is given in 37B and 37C.

THE HASMONEANS

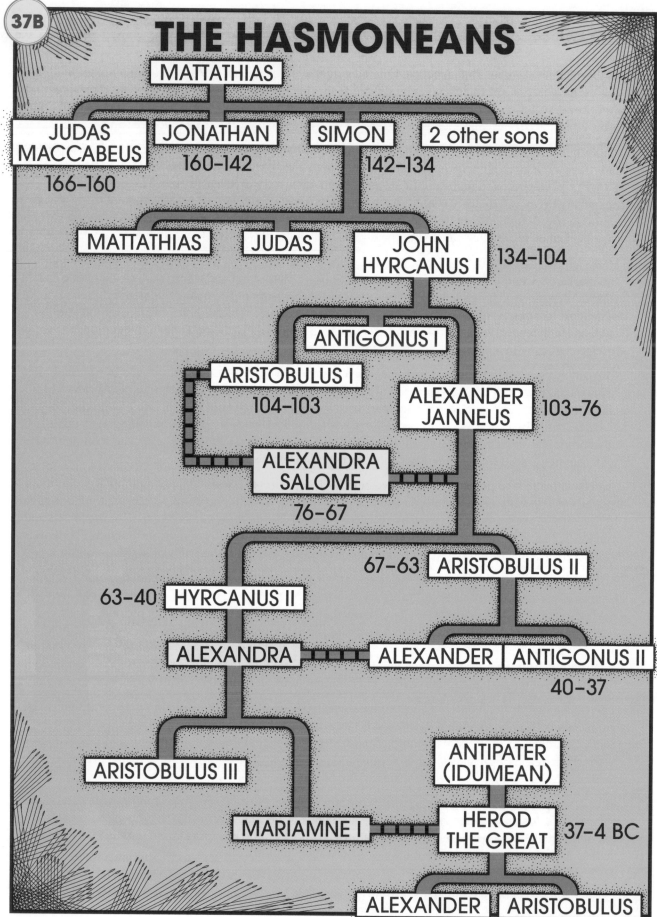

Note: *Christian writers usually use the term "Hasmonean" to refer to John Hyrcanus' descendants. Jewish writers include all the Maccabees under this term. What follows is a summary of succession in relation to the period of rule by the Maccabees and Hasmoneans. The more brutal events associated with campaigns and transfer of power will be dealt with in Section 37C. The information that follows in 37B is derived from 1 and 2 Maccabees and the writings of the Jewish historian, Josephus (ca. A.D. 37–100).*

1 *MATTATHIAS* Hasmoneas, a Jewish priest, triggered an incident that resulted in a revolt against Antiochus IV "Epiphanes". His five sons played an important role in the revolt. Two of his sons, John and Eleazar, are not listed by name in the illustration.

2 *JUDAS MACCABEUS* ("The Hammer") assumed control of the revolt in *166* B.C. He was killed in battle in *160* B.C.

3 *JONATHAN* (Mattathias' fifth son) then took over until he was assassinated in *142* B.C.

4 *SIMON* (Mattathias' second son) followed Jonathan.

5 Simon's son, *JOHN HYRCANUS*, then took control and ruled until *104* B.C.

6 John Hyrcanus was succeeded by two of his three sons. First, *ARISTOBULUS I* ruled for one year, *104–103* B.C. *ALEXANDER JANNAEUS* then ruled for 27 years, *103–76* B.C.

7 After Aristobulus died, his widow, *ALEXANDRA SALOME*, married Alexander Jannaeus.

8 After Alexander Jannaeus' death in 76 B.C., Alexandra Salome succeeded him to the throne. *HYRCANUS II*, the older of her two sons, served as High Priest during her reign.

9 It was Alexandra Salome's wish that Hyrcanus II succeed her as king. However, after her death *ARISTOBULUS II*, her other son, immediately marched against his older brother Hyrcanus and sent him fleeing to Jerusalem—where he surrendered and renounced the throne in favor of Aristobulus, asking only for the freedom to enjoy his revenues.

10 However, the Idumean ruler *ANTIPATER* (father of Herod the Great) appeared on the scene, convincing many Jews that Aristobulus had no lawful right to the throne. He secured a safe haven for Hyrcanus in Petra, capital of the Nabatean king Aretas.

11 Hyrcanus promised Aretas a dozen cities to the east and south of the Dead Sea in return for an army to deal with his brother, Aristobulus. The Nabatean forces defeated Aristobulus and drove him into the fortified Temple Mount in Jerusalem. Only the priestly party remained loyal to Aristobulus.

12 Enter the Romans! Although fighting continued between the two "brotherly factions," with each seeking the support of the Romans, there came the day when Pompey confirmed Hyrcanus II as High Priest, but did not give him a royal title.

13 Hyrcanus' daughter, *ALEXANDRA* (who married *ALEXANDER*, a son of Aristobulus II), produced two children, *ARISTOBULUS III* and *MARIAMNE*. Mariamne eventually married *HEROD THE GREAT*, a son of the Idumean Antipater. Their two sons, *ALEXANDER* and *ARISTOBULUS*, vied for power in Judea—but were eventually strangled at the order of their father, Herod. Herod also had Mariamne's brother, Aristobulus III, drowned.

THE HASMONEAN STATE: BORDERS & RULERS

142 B.C. ▦ Independent Judea

104 B.C. ▦ Expanded Hasmonean state

76 B.C. ▦ Further expanded Hasmonean state

SYRIA

PHOENICIA

GAULANITIS

Antiochia

Tyre

Seleucia

Ptolemais

Bascama

Taricheae

SEA OF GALILEE

Sepphoris

GALILEE

Dora Mt. Tabor

Gadara

Strato's Tower

GILEAD

Scythopolis

Pella

SAMARIA

Samaria Shechem

Gerasa

Apollonia

Mt. Gerizim

Jordan River

AMMONITIS

Joppa

Arimathea

PEREA

Lydda Dok Jericho

Modein

Qumran

Jerusalem

JUDAH

Azotus

Hycania

Ascalon

Marisa

Hebron

Gaza

IDUMEA

Machaerus

DEAD SEA

Raphia Beer-sheba

Masada

MOABITIS

Rhinocorura

Zoar

† x 800

BORDERS

1 *142 B.C.* Although Judas Maccabeus and his supporters managed to cleanse and rededicate the Jerusalem Temple in 164 B.C., the regions of Judah and Perea remained under Seleucid control. In **ILLUSTRATION 37C**, the dotted yellow segment depicts the territory the Seleucids declared to be an independent Jewish state in the spring of 142 B.C. during the reign of Mattathias' third son, Simon.

2 *104 B.C.* When, in 134 B.C., Simon and two of his sons were assassinated in the fortress of Dok to the west of Jericho, John Hyrcanus, his surviving son, succeeded him. He began to expand Judah's borders, accelerating the rise of the Hasmonean kingdom. The territory he added to his realm by the year 104 B.C. is depicted in **ILLUSTRATION 37C** by the green segments with vertical stripes.

3 *76 B.C.* John Hyrcanus was succeeded by his son, Aristobulus, who ruled for only one year. Aristobulus' brother and successor, Alexander Jannaeus, launched a series of military campaigns that greatly increased the size of his kingdom. (In **ILLUSTRATION 37C**, the regions he added to his realm are depicted in orange with sloping stripes.) By the time of his death in 76 B.C., the nation's borders almost matched those of David's realm.

RULERS

1 *Mattathias Hasmoneas*, who initiated the revolt against Antiochus IV "Epiphanes", was a priest (***priest's hat***). The revolt he instigated was a political venture (***small crown***) designed to cleanse the Jerusalem Temple of Hellenistic practices and to restore the observance of proper worship and ritual within the Temple and throughout Judah. After his death, the uprising he instigated was perpetuated by ***three of his five sons***.

2 *Judas Maccabeus*, Mattathias' ***third son***, led the uprising until he was killed in battle in 160 B.C. Because of his leadership role in the attempt to eliminate Seleucid control and influence by force of arms (***sword***), he was given the nickname Maccabeus ("The ***Hammer***").

Judas succeeded in assembling a guerilla group that dealt with the Syrian forces sent into Palestine to crush the revolt. Fortunately for Judas, Antiochus was occupied in the eastern part of his realm fighting the Parthians, which limited the size of the force that could be dispatched against Judas. After repulsing a Syrian attack led by Lysias, Judas boldly determined to rid the Temple of the "abomination of desolation" that Antiochus had placed within it. The priest Menelaus was still in control of the Temple. However, in 165 B.C., Judas' men captured Jerusalem, cleansed the Temple of all traces of the pagan cult, and shut up the Seleucid garrison and the Jews who supported Antiochus in the Acra fortress. The cleansed Temple and altar were then rededicated and restored to proper use. The event was celebrated for eight days, and is still recalled and celebrated in the annual Feast of Hanukkah. Judas' victory had wiped out three years of blasphemy.

Although the Maccabean revolt had achieved a major objective, it did not end here. The rebels' success encouraged them to struggle even more for full political independence. The plan was to extend Maccabean power and influence. They began by rescuing Jewish minority groups scattered throughout Judah and the Transjordan and bringing them to Jerusalem.

After Antiochus IV "Epiphanes" died in 163 B.C., his eight-year-old son, Antiochus V, succeeded him. In that same year, Judas undertook to destroy the Syrian fortress (Acra) in Jerusalem, but Syrian reinforcements came to its rescue and besieged the Maccabeans in Jerusalem. The situation looked hopeless. Fortunately, the Syrian general Lysias had to return home to preserve his own authority as regent of the young king and was compelled to draw up a treaty that granted the Jews the right to follow their own laws, 1 Maccabees 6:59. Although the Maccabees had now achieved their primary goal, the temptation to gain greater independence and political power remained. Their troubles were far from over.

In Syria, both Antiochus V and Lysias were murdered. The new king was Demetrius I, a son of Seleucus IV. The Hellenistic Jews in Judah opposed Judas and appealed to Demetrius for protection against him. Demetrius appointed their candidate, Alcimus, as High Priest (*priest's hat*). Division among the Jews resulted. The Hasidim, who earlier had supported Judas, accepted Alcimus—who was of legitimate priestly descent. Judas opposed Alcimus, who then appealed to Syria for help. Several battles resulted. When faced by a vastly superior army, many of Judas' supporters deserted him. The Jews were routed and Judas was killed.

3 Mattathias' *fifth son*, *Jonathan*, took Judas' place. Alcimus remained in office, and the Jewish people retained their freedom of worship. A shift in thinking took place in the minds of many Jews. Although some continued to support the Maccabees, the Hasidim believed that, since religious freedom had been restored, enough had been achieved. Their interest was religious—not political.

Jonathan led the Maccabean movement until 143 B.C. He undertook only limited campaigns, and operated in the style of the ancient judges (*small crown*) from his base at Michmash, seven miles northeast of Jerusalem. The high priest Alcimus died in 159 B.C. and was not replaced for some years.

The day came when a tempting offer was made to Jonathan. In 153 B.C., Alexander Balas, a pretender to the Syrian throne and claiming to be a son of Antiochus IV, landed at Ptolemais and challenged Demetrius I. Demetrius authorized Jonathan to assemble an army, but Alexander Balas offered Jonathan the office of High Priest in return for his support. Although Jonathan did not belong to the Zadokite line, he accepted the offer (*priest's hat*)—and Alexander Balas triumphed. Further honors came Jonathan's way. Alexander invited Jonathan to Acre to attend his marriage to a daughter of Ptolemy VI. While there, Jonathan was clothed in purple and appointed the governor of Judea.

The Maccabees now had more power than ever, and were in a position to play the Seleucid kings against each other. Dynastic struggles continued in Syria. Demetrius II slew Alexander Balas and took the throne. Demetrius was challenged by Antiochus VI, who was supported by a certain Trypho. Trypho, who hoped to gain the Seleucid throne for himself, saw in Jonathan a dangerous rival, took him prisoner through an act of treachery, and put him to death (*dagger*) at Bascama on the northeast corner of the Sea of Galilee.

4 *Simon*, Mattathias' second son, succeeded Jonathan and ruled from 143–134 B.C. Simon supported Demetrius II, who in turn recognized Simon as High Priest (*priest's hat*), granted him exemption from tax, and acknowledged the independence and sovereignty of Judah. The Jews now began to date contracts and agreements from 142 B.C., "the first year of Simon the great High Priest, and commander and leader of the Jews," 1 Maccabees 13:41,42. (Note: *commander* and *leader* (*small crown*), but not yet king.) In the following year, Simon gained control of the Acra fortress in Jerusalem—the last stronghold of foreign domination. Some years of peace followed.

Eventually, yet another rival claimant to the Syrian throne arose, namely Antiochus Sidetes. Simon refused to yield to his demands, and in the battle that followed, his two sons conquered Antiochus' general. But tragedy followed. Simon and two of his sons visited Simon's son-in-law, Ptolemy (an Egyptian name but not an Egyptian ruler), at the fortress of Dok near Jericho. Ptolemy killed all three guests (*3 daggers*), hoping to make himself king.

5 However, *John*—another of Simon's sons and the administrator of Gazara—hurried to Jerusalem before Ptolemy arrived there, and had himself installed as Priest-Prince (*priest's hat, small crown*) under the throne name of John Hyrcanus I (*Hyrcanus*, a Greek name), and ruled 134–104 B.C.

[First Maccabees ends its account at this point. The source for continuing information is the Jewish historian, Josephus.]

Hyrcanus tried to punish Ptolemy, but the latter fled. Hyrcanus' first years were difficult ones.

Antiochus VII ravaged Judah and set siege to Jerusalem. The Romans forced him to lift the siege, but in the treaty that followed, Hyrcanus was forced to pay tribute to Antiochus, and Judah became a vassal province. The independence gained under Judas and Jonathan now seemed lost.

A turn for the better took place after Antiochus was killed in battle in 128 B.C. While his successor, Demetrius II, was involved in civil war, Hyrcanus conquered and regained considerable territory, destroyed the Samaritan temple on Mt. Gerizim, and captured Samaria in 107 B.C. Hyrcanus had succeeded in making his realm an important military power in the region. In the style of other Hellenistic rulers, Hyrcanus minted coins upon which were embossed his name and Greek fertility symbols.

However, all was not well. Hyrcanus was opposed by the Pharisees—the spiritual descendants of the Hasidim. Their opposition continued until the dynasty finally fell. The Pharisees accused the Hasmoneans of profaning the office of High Priest out of a desire for military and secular power.

There was truth to the charges of the Pharisees. Although the Maccabean uprising began as a revolt against persecution, and out of a desire to defend Judaism against the inroads of Hellenism, the leaders of the movement became something of a Hellenistic princely dynasty themselves. A clash between Hyrcanus and the Pharisees was inevitable.

Although the Sadducean party (consisting of priests and nobles) should have felt unhappy about a Maccabee as High Priest, they tolerated the situation and allied themselves to the Hasmoneans to gain influence in the realm.

6 John Hyrcanus decreed that, after his death, his widow was to succeed him as political ruler and his son *Aristobulus* was to serve as High Priest. However, Aristobulus imprisoned his mother and two brothers, Antigonus and Alexander Jannaeus (***three figures behind bars***)—and permitted his mother to starve to death. Aristobulus, already High Priest (***priest's hat***), was the first to take the royal title "King" (***larger crown***) instead of "ethnarch," or "ruler of a people." His successors continued to use this title until 63 B.C. Although the Pharisees objected, saying that only a descendant of David could take this title, Aristobulus ignored their objections. He died in 103 B.C. after ruling for only one year.

7 After Aristobulus' death, his widow *Salome Alexandra* freed his two brothers from prison, installed one of them—*Alexander Jannaeus*—as High Priest-King (***priest's hat, larger crown***), and married him. Jannaeus ruled 103–76 B.C. Many of his subjects hated him. In about 90 B.C., when trying to expand his realm to the northeast, he was defeated by the Nabateans, and lost his entire army in the process. His defeat sparked a rebellion led by the Pharisees. After crushing the revolt in a brutal manner, Jannaeus crucified 800 Pharisees in front of his palace in Jerusalem, where he and the women of his harem (while enjoying a banquet together) could watch them die in agony. When his dissolute life came to an end in 76 B.C., his death was greeted with great joy by his subjects. Even so, he had carved out for himself a realm whose boundaries were only a little less than those of David's kingdom.

8 *Salome Alexandra* succeeded her husband as queen (***larger crown***), 76–67 B.C. She managed to bring order to her realm, and made peace with the Pharisees. Salome had ***two sons***—the mild Hyrcanus II and Aristobulus II, who was as vicious as his father. She made her oldest son, Hyrcanus II, High Priest (***priest's hat***), and stated that it was her wish that he eventually succeed her as King and High Priest.

9 After Salome Alexandra's death, *Hyrcanus* and *Aristobulus* fought for control (***sword***). A bitter and complicated struggle ensued—with Aristobulus emerging the victor (***priest's hat, larger crown***). Hyrcanus obtained Nabatean help, besieged Jerusalem, and would have regained control but for one factor.

10 In 63 B.C., *Rome* intervened (***Roman helmet and sword***). Each claimant appealed to Pompey for a decision in his favor. When Aristobulus refused to hand over the Temple to Pompey, the latter besieged Jerusalem. After the city fell to Pompey, he killed many, entered the Temple's Holy of Holies (a sacrilege that pious Jews never forgot!), restored the offering of Jewish sacrifices, imprisoned Aristobulus, and agreed to the appointment of Hyrcanus as High Priest (***priest's hat***).

The real power behind Hyrcanus was Antipater from Idumea. The Idumeans, descendants of the Edomites, had been forcibly converted to Judaism by John Hyrcanus I. According to the Jewish historian Josephus, Antipater had married a woman named Cypros of an illustrious Arab (probably Nabatean) family. When Julius Caesar supplanted Pompey as Roman leader, he appointed Antipater as procurator of Judea (the Roman name for Judah).

Judea, now part of the Roman province of Syria, was forced to pay tribute to Rome. The independence the Maccabees had gained came to an end. The territories that Simon, John Hyrcanus, and Alexander Jannaeus had added to the realm were lost. The region that the Jerusalem High Priest controlled was greatly reduced in size. Things now looked very different indeed.

Roman Rule

1 Hyrcanus II held office from 63 until 40 B.C. Alexander, a son of Aristobulus, tried to wrest power from him, but was prevented from doing so by the Romans. Meanwhile, Antipater (who had helped Hyrcanus plan the siege of Jerusalem against Aristobulus) was gaining increasing influence in Jerusalem and was all but running the administration for the ineffective Hyrcanus.

2 In 49 B.C., Julius Caesar crossed the Rubicon. Pompey, his rival, was forced to flee to the east. At first Hyrcanus and Antipater sided with Pompey, but after reading the writing on the wall, they threw in their lot with Caesar. Caesar eventually bestowed on Hyrcanus the title of Ethnarch and confirmed him in the position of High Priest. Antipater was given Roman citizenship and made procurator of Judea. Antipater made two of his sons governors: Phasael over Jerusalem, and Herod over Galilee. Herod's success in this position led the Roman senate to appoint him as king of Judea in 40 B.C.

3 Caesar was assassinated in 44 B.C. The Jews lamented the event. His assassins fled east and Cassius took over control of Syria. Antipater and his son Herod supported him. However, in 43 B.C., Hyrcanus' cup-bearer poisoned Antipater. To bind the Hasmonean and Idumean families closer together, Hyrcanus gave his granddaughter Mariamne to Herod in marriage in 37 B.C.

4 Cassius exploited the region, but was finally defeated by Mark Antony and Octavian at Philippi. Because Roman control over Syria was weak at this time, the Parthians were able to invade it in 40 B.C. With Parthian backing, Antigonus, the son of Aristobulus II and nephew of Hyrcanus II, gained the office of High Priest and remained in office from 40 to 37 B.C.

5 Antigonus captured Phasael and Hyrcanus II through trickery, and cut off the latter's ears—thus making it impossible for him to hold office as High Priest, Leviticus 21:16–23. Phasael committed suicide. His brother Herod fled to Rome where he won the favor of Octavian and Mark Antony. They declared him "King of Judea," but left it to him to conquer his kingdom. He achieved this three years later with Roman help. Hasmonean power now came to an end. Herod, an Idumean married to the granddaughter of Hyrcanus, ascended the Judean throne and ruled the realm 37–4 B.C.

Herod the Great

1 Herod had received a good education in the art of political survival from his father, Antipater. While serving as governor of Galilee and after putting to death a bandit leader, the Jerusalem Sanhedrin summoned him to Jerusalem to stand trial for murder. Although Herod was expected to appear before the Sanhedrin with a humble demeanor and dressed in dark robes, he arrived dressed in lavish purple robes, accompanied by his bodyguards. Hyrcanus called off the trial, and advised Herod to leave the city.

2 Herod found refuge with the Roman governor in Damascus who put him in charge of southern Syria and gave him the governorship of Samaria, Galilee, and Coelesyria. When the Parthians invaded Herod's territory in 40 B.C. and placed the Hasmonean, Antigonus, on the throne, Herod first sought refuge at Masada, then fled to Rome to seek help, returned to Palestine, gathered an army, rescued his relatives at Masada, and finally, with Roman help, captured Jerusalem in 37 B.C. Contrary to Herod's wishes, the Romans devastated the city, slaughtered many of its citizens, and executed Antigonus.

3 Many Jewish leaders had supported Antigonus. Herod had hundreds killed and seized their estates— thereby adding greatly to his own wealth. Among the victims were 45 members of the Jerusalem nobility, most of whom were members of the Sanhedrin. Herod then packed the Sanhedrin with his own followers. His advisers were Greeks. His army consisted largely of foreign mercenaries. He developed a secret police and a network of spies to report to him from every corner of his realm.

4 Herod became extremely wealthy. Revenues poured in from his vast estates, from high-priced loans to foreign rulers, from his own shrewd business dealings, and from high taxation. Most of this wealth flowed into a building program of gigantic proportions. He put up monuments as though he himself were the emperor. The buildings and gardens of the palace-fortress, the Herodium, covered 45 acres, making it one of the largest royal buildings in the ancient world. He built three palaces in Jericho (one of which became his favorite home), two atop Masada, and others at Ascalon, Sepphoris, Machaerus, Jerusalem, and elsewhere. He created two new cities at Sebaste (ancient Samaria, renamed to honor the Emperor) and Caesarea (formerly Strato's Tower). Caesarea, which became the kingdom's first true seaport, was built around an artificial harbor protected by massive breakwaters. Abraham's traditional burial place at Mamre (Hebron) was enclosed with massive masonry.

5 Herod turned Jerusalem itself into a Greco-Roman city. The rebuilding project began soon after Herod took office and continued until well after his death. The work gave steady employment to thousands of craftsmen and common laborers, and turned the city into an international showplace. Among Herod's Jerusalem projects were the fortress of Antonia, an enormous palace in the elite western sector of the Upper City, a theater, an amphitheater, a hippodrome, parks, gardens, and fountains. Finally, in 19 B.C., Herod began the restoration and embellishment of the Second Temple. The central structure was soon completed, but work on its precincts was completed only about A.D. 63—seven years before its final destruction by the Romans.

6 Most of those who had achieved power and prestige under Herod belonged to the priestly families that had been absent from Judea since the Babylonian exile. Not only had these families played a leading role among the communities of the Diaspora, but they had also mingled with the rich and powerful of the Greek and Roman worlds, and had absorbed cosmopolitan attitudes and tastes. These influential people became part of Herod's realm either because Herod encouraged them to return, or because his expanding borders engulfed them. They found themselves feeling more at home among the members of Herod's court than among those who had maintained Judea's traditions for centuries. The control of the Temple and priesthood passed into their hands.

7 In about 23 B.C., Herod appointed the highly respected Simon ben Boethus from Alexandria to the position of High Priest, and shortly afterward married his daughter—another Mariamne. Simon remained in office until 4 B.C. (the year of Herod's death) when Herod, suspecting Mariamne of plotting against him, divorced her, and replaced her father. Simon's replacement soon lost his position, as did his replacement, who was followed in rapid succession by two of Simon's sons, Joezer and Eleazar. A third son, Simon, later held the position under direct Roman authority. This chaotic series of events sowed the seeds for a new elite among the High Priests, their families, and their descendants.

8 Herod had surrounded himself with philosophers and academics as advisors. His closest advisor and confidant, Nicolaus, came from the ancient but thoroughly Hellenized city of Damascus. He had received a full Greek education in the arts and sciences, and embraced the philosophy of Aristotle. A scholar with an international reputation, he had been a tutor in the court of Antony and Cleopatra, and transferred to Herod's employment after their deaths.

9 At heart, Herod was a Hellenist and displayed little interest in Judaism. He was a king of the Jews but certainly not a Jewish king. All ranks and designations at Herod's court were Greek-inspired—including the official playmates for the royal children. Coins were inscribed in Greek rather than in Hebrew. Greek names were common among the Jewish upper classes. The kingdom's chief financial minister, who had charge of the king's signet ring, was named Ptolemy.

10 Herod's military forces were composed largely of mercenaries. His personal bodyguard was a company of 400 well-trained Galatians given him by Emperor Augustus. There were also regiments of local Jewish conscripts and militiamen whom Herod rewarded with grants of farmlands, or settled in military colonies along his borders. At one point, he added to his army more than 500 cavalrymen from Babylonia, all crack shots with bow and arrow, installed them in their own new city in a key border province in the northeast, and made their land a tax-free zone—which in turn attracted other colonists.

11 Herod's subjects hated him; to them he was only a half-Jew. His various appointments were unacceptable to the Pharisees who on two occasions refused to swear allegiance to Herod and the emperor. In Herod's Palestine, the strength of Hellenism confronted the strength of Judaism and the confrontation was never far from explosive. The resulting animosity moved Herod to resort to violence to keep his subjects under control.

12 The last years of Herod's reign were marked by domestic strife. For all his political skill, he was never able to control his family, many of whom had egos as immense as his own. Herod had at various times married a total of ten wives, and, as might be expected, the atmosphere of the court became poisoned by the competition among them, with the result that he saw fit to repudiate some of them, together with their children.

13 Herod's first wife, Doris, bore him a son named Antipater (named after Herod's father, Antipater II). Herod eventually divorced Doris and married Mariamne, the granddaughter of the Hasmonean High Priest, Hyrcanus II. But when Mariamne's mother, Alexandra, successfully conspired through Antony and Cleopatra to have Mariamne's 17-year-old brother, Aristobulus III, appointed High Priest in place of Herod's appointee, Herod recognized a clear challenge to his rule—with the result that the new appointee "accidentally" drowned while swimming with some young noblemen at the old Hasmonean palace in Jericho. This was the first of a series of family murders and executions. The next victim was Mariamne's grandfather, Hyrcanus II, who was strangled. Shortly thereafter, Mariamne, who had denied Herod access to her bed, was put to death. Even so, Herod sent Mariamne's two sons, Aristobulus and Alexander, to Rome to be properly educated. After putting Mariamne I to death, Herod married a beautiful Jewess of the same name, Mariamne, who bore him Herod Philip.

14 Augustus had given Herod the right to name his own successor. The chief contenders were Antipater (by his first wife, Doris, a native of Jerusalem) and the two Hasmonean brothers, Alexander and Aristobulus—sons of Mariamne I. The latter turned out to be arrogant and abusive, openly deriding Herod and the Idumean side of the family. Antipater, in turn, was sly and sharp and did everything he could to poison Herod's mind against Alexander and Aristobulus—with the result that Herod finally named Antipater crown prince, and Alexander and Aristobulus second and third in line. When Herod uncovered a plot indicating that the two Hasmonean brothers were plotting to kill him, he had them strangled. And when news reached Herod's ears that Antipater was plotting to hasten his father's death, Herod had him imprisoned in the Hyrcania fortress, on the northwest corner of the Dead Sea.

15 During Herod's final and painful illness, a rumor spread that he had already died before this actually was the case. Two rabbis urged the people to tear down the golden eagle from the gate of the Temple in Jerusalem (Herod had it placed there). Herod responded by ordering the rabbis to be burned alive. Fearing that his death would not be mourned, Herod commanded that notable Jews from all parts of the land come to him—and had them confined in the city's hippodrome. He then gave orders that, upon his death, all of them were to be killed so that wails of grief would be heard throughout the realm. (However, it was not carried out.) It was his second to last executive command. Five days before his death, Herod told some of his bodyguards to kill his imprisoned son, Antipater. When Caesar Augustus was informed of Antipater's death, he reportedly remarked, "It is better to be Herod's pig than his son."

16 According to Herod's final will, Archelaus, son of his fourth wife, Malthace of Samaria, was to reign over the bulk of his territory. The remainder of his realm was to be divided among two other surviving sons. Herod Philip, son of Herod's fifth wife (Cleopatra), was to rule the Transjordanian lands of Batanea and Trachonitis. Herod Antipas, another son of Malthace, was to rule Galilee and Perea. This arrangement was ratified by the Roman Emperor, Augustus. However, Augustus withheld the title of king from Herod's successors; there was to be no danger of their claiming independence from Rome.

17 Herod died at Jericho in 4 B.C. and was buried in the Herodium fortress a few miles southeast of Bethlehem. Few mourned Herod's passing. He is remembered today mostly because of what is recorded in Matthew 2:1, "In the time of King Herod, Jesus was born in Bethlehem of Judea."

37A Cyrus of Persia overthrew the Babylonians in 538 B.C. Little is known about his successors. The Greeks under Alexander the Great conquered the Persians in 332 B.C. After Alexander's death in 323 B.C., his realm was divided among his generals. Ptolemy and his successors ruled Egypt. Seleucus and his successors ruled in the Fertile Crescent. The Ptolemies controlled Palestine until 198 B.C., when they lost it to the Seleucids.

The Seleucid Antiochus IV "Epiphanes" ruled from 175 to 163 B.C. He made strenuous efforts to enforce Hellenism throughout his realm and resorted to violent measures to stamp out Judaism, which he saw as a hindrance to his dream. In 168 B.C., he desecrated the Jerusalem Temple and began an organized persecution of the Jews. A revolt broke out under the leadership of the Maccabees. Eventually, under the leadership of Judas Maccabeus (Judas the Hammer), the Maccabees defeated the Syrian forces, and cleansed and rededicated the Temple in December 165 B.C.

37B The history of the Maccabees/Hasmoneans is complex—and brutal. Judas Maccabeus died in battle. His brothers and successors, Jonathan and Simon, were both assassinated. The goal of those who succeeded them was to restore Judah's borders to what they had been during David's day. Alexander Jannaeus assassinated vast numbers of those who opposed him and his rule. His wife, Alexandra Salome, who succeeded him and proved a moderate ruler. However, after her death, her two sons battled each other to gain access to the throne. And then in 63 B.C., the Romans took over control of Judah—and renamed it Judea (a Roman name). Eventually, in 37 B.C., Herod the Great—an Idumean (a descendant of Esau)—gained access to the throne of Judea and ruled under the watchful eye of his Roman overlords. Herod's second wife was Mariamne, a Hasmonean princess. However, Herod eventually had Mariamne, her two sons by Herod, and her brother Aristobolus put to death. Herod saw all four as power-hungry and a threat to his authority.

37C The Maccabean movement became one motivated by dynastic and territorial ambition. It gave birth to a dynasty in which the ruler served as both High Priest and political leader. After Rome rose to power and took over control of the eastern Mediterranean world in 63 B.C., Herod the Great ruled Judea, Samaria, Galilee, Perea, and Gaulanitis with Roman sanction from 37–4 B.C. When Herod died in 4 B.C., his remains were interred in the Herodium fortress/palace a few miles southeast of Bethlehem, Jesus' birthplace.

Those who wish to understand the New Testament fully need to make themselves familiar with the contents of the Old Testament and with the history of the intertestamental period—in particular, that of the Maccabees, Hasmoneans, and Herod the Great.

CROSS WAYS

4
SECTION

UNITS 31–40
The Postexilic Period
and Judaism

UNIT 38
Apocalyptic and Daniel

The Nature of Apocalyptic Literature;
The Message of Daniel to a Persecuted Judah

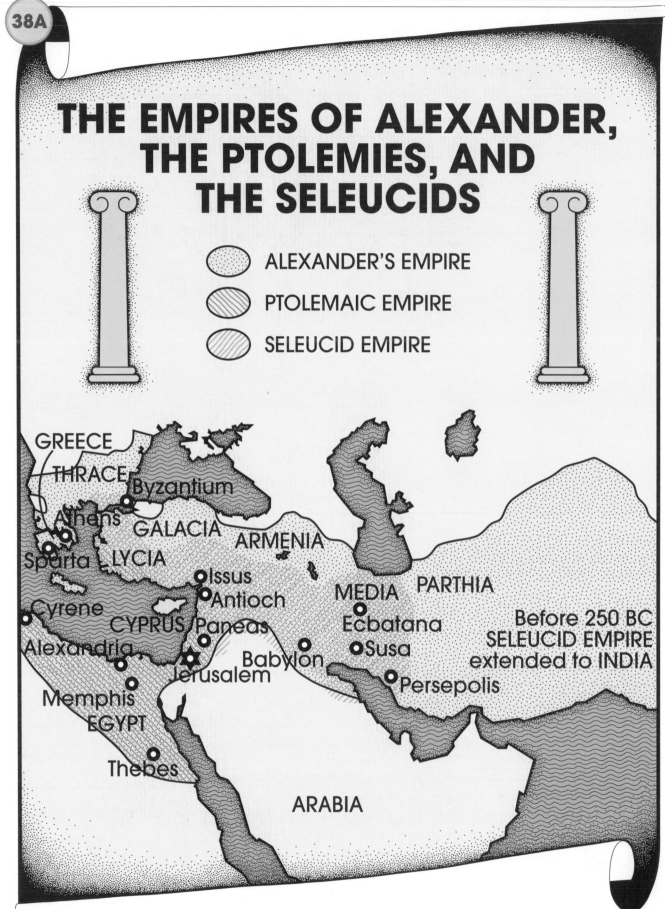

THE EMPIRES OF ALEXANDER, THE PTOLEMIES, AND THE SELEUCIDS

ALEXANDER'S EMPIRE

PTOLEMAIC EMPIRE

SELEUCID EMPIRE

GREECE
THRACE
Byzantium
Athens
GALACIA
ARMENIA
Sparta LYCIA
Issus
Antioch MEDIA PARTHIA
Cyrene CYPRUS Paneas
Ecbatana Before 250 BC
Alexandria Susa SELEUCID EMPIRE
Babylon extended to INDIA
Jerusalem
Persepolis
Memphis
EGYPT
Thebes
ARABIA

Enter Hellenism

ILLUSTRATION 38A sets the stage for the historical situation to which the book of Daniel speaks.

1 *ALEXANDER'S EMPIRE:* During the period 333–323 B.C., Alexander the Great established a vast empire. He did not live to rule it, for he died at **Babylon** in 323 B.C. when returning from military ventures to the east—in what today is Pakistan and India.

2 After Alexander's death, his empire was divided among his generals. Ptolemy took control of Egypt (**PTOLEMAIC EMPIRE**), and Seleucus took control of Babylonia (**SELEUCID EMPIRE**). During the period 323–301 B.C., Judah changed hands five times. Ptolemy entered Judah in 312 B.C. to incorporate it into his realm, and completed the venture in 301 B.C.

3 Seleucus established his new capital at **Antioch** on the Orontes River. One of his successors, Antiochus III, managed to conquer Syria and surrounding territories, including Judah, by 198 B.C. The Jews fared well under the new administration. The Seleucids permitted them to live under their own laws, financed the cost of the sacrifices required in the **Jerusalem** Temple, and kept the Temple structure in good repair. The nation's elders, and Jerusalem's Temple staff and residents, enjoyed financial privileges.

4 After the death of Antiochus III, the Seleucid empire began to decline. Dynastic strife broke out. Seleucus IV, Antiochus' son and successor, ruled from 185 until 175 B.C. Eventually another son of Antiochus III gained the throne. The new king, Antiochus IV, adopted the title "Epiphanes" (Manifestation), believing that the god Zeus was manifest in him. His subjects responded by nicknaming him "Epimanes" (madman).

5 Antiochus had two main goals. The *first* was to restore the borders of his realm to what they had been at the time of Alexander the Great. The *second* was to introduce the culture of Hellenism (**Greek columns**) into all corners of his realm, *including Judah*, to unite it. Hellenism focused on the concept of wisdom, and encouraged people to seek it. Other Hellenistic elements related to religion and worship, dress, games, architecture, and language.

A key reason for Antiochus wanting to expand his borders and unify its cultural and religious practices was the threat of the growing power of Rome. He wanted a united realm that was sufficiently powerful to deal with Rome's growing political ambitions.

6 After returning from his first campaign in **EGYPT** (169 B.C.), Antiochus entered and plundered the Jerusalem Temple to obtain funds to help finance his military campaigns. When he undertook a second campaign against Egypt in 168 B.C., Popilius of Rome ordered him to terminate the campaign immediately.

7 Repressive measures against the Jews followed. An official persecution began. The Torah was declared invalid. The offering of sacrifices in the Temple was forbidden, as were rites of circumcision, the observance of food laws and annual feasts, and Sabbath observance. The practice of these rites was viewed as political treason and disloyalty to Seleucid rule. The penalty for their observance was death. Eventually *the abomination of desolation* (an altar to Olympian Zeus) was placed in the Jerusalem Temple. Altars were also set up in other parts of the country; all citizens were expected to offer sacrifices and pledge allegiance to Antiochus at these altars. The challenge and choice confronting Jews was now clear.

THE PROPHETIC APPEAL

'Repent!'

THE FUTURE

1

THE APOCALYPTIC APPEAL

MESSIANIC AGE

'Stand firm! Trust!'

2

PSEUDONYMOUS APOCALYPTIC

AUTHOR
pretends to be here

AUTHOR
is really here

PAST EVENTS PRESENTED
AS PREDICTIONS
(relatively accurate)

PREDICTIONS
(relatively inaccurate)

3

A Comparison of Literary Genres

➊ THE PROPHETIC APPEAL

Old Testament prophets (*male figure with raised hands*) based their message on the *covenant* God made with the Israelites at *Mt. Sinai.*

The prophets charged the nation with ignoring and breaking the stipulations of the Sinai covenant (*shattered covenant*), and warned the people that the covenant curses would soon overtake them. *THE FUTURE* of the nation was in question. Doom loomed on the horizon.

There was still time—but only a very short time! If the nation sincerely *repented* and returned to the Lord, the relationship between God and the people could be set right, and the threatening doom averted. A key word in the prophetic message was *'Repent!'*

➋ THE APOCALYPTIC APPEAL

The apocalyptic appeal was different. The problem was not the nation's sin, but the fact that the nation was in bondage to a foreign oppressor (*circle of chains*), and was suffering at its hands (*sword*). The nation appeared helpless, and the situation looked hopeless.

However, the writer assured his readers that God (*symbol for God*) would soon break in to their situation to destroy their oppressor and deliver them (*broken sword, broken chains*).

Within a short time, the evil situation would be over and the *MESSIANIC AGE* would break in. All this would come about, not as a result of any *human repentance* (the problem was not the people's sin!), but as a result of *divine intervention* by God Himself. The appeal was *'Stand firm! Trust!'*

➌ PSEUDONYMOUS AUTHORSHIP

Writers of apocalyptic literature often (but not always) used a pseudonym (pen-name) when writing. There was good reason for this. Apocalyptic literature is underground, resistance writing. It was written at a time when the nation was in danger. The oppressor was making life intolerable and would tolerate no opposition. It was essential that the writer keep his identity secret, lest he lose his life.

Hence it became common practice for the writer to *pretend* to be a well-known *ancient* figure, writing *predictively* about the deliverance *that was soon to take place.* When speaking about events leading up to the situation of the moment, his so-called "predictions" could be reasonably accurate.

However, predictions about events beyond the immediate present could be inaccurate. The writer's concern went beyond the realm of historical accuracy to the desire to speak meaningfully to colleagues facing the threat of death.

21st Century Style...

1 You live on an island in a troubled part of the world. The island is small and has a population of about one thousand people. All are Christians and hold membership in the one church located in the center of the island's one town.

2 You wake up one morning to face a challenge. During the night, troops from a nearby nation have invaded the island. They are well-armed, well-positioned, and have taken over a building as their headquarters across the square from your church. Some of them occupy the church itself and have replaced its altar with an altar on which is a pagan image.

3 You are no longer permitted to possess or read a Bible. You are told that if you baptize your child, you and the child will be killed. You are forbidden to take part in any Christian observances. The ruler of the occupying nation insists that your community revere him as the incarnation of the deity, as "the *Inspired* One." (You quip that he is "the *Insane* One.") He commands that a dog be offered in sacrifice on the pagan altar now located in your church. He also insists that all eat a piece of cooked dog to indicate submission to his rule. Finally, the Inspired One declares that it is his goal to rule the world and have all people conform to the cultural traditions of his realm.

4 How would you and your fellow citizens meet the situation? If you rose up in open revolt, you would be wiped out immediately. You cannot shout protests in the town square, for a bullet would bring your speech to a swift conclusion. Most likely, you and other loyalists would go underground. To encourage opposition to the occupying forces, you would produce an underground newspaper. In it you would publish stories meaningful to those on *your side*, but unintelligible to those on the *other side*. You would not sign your real name to any article, but use a pen name, a *nom-de-plume*. To illustrate, if all living on the island were Americans, you might sign your name as "Paul Bunyan," or "Betsy Ross," and tell stories about incidents in America's *past* that spoke to your community's *present*. The punchline of the articles would be: "Do not yield! Stand firm! Deliverance will come soon!"

Unit 38 analyzes the book of Daniel as "underground literature," written to urge pious Jews to remain loyal to the faith of their fathers during the persecution of Antiochus IV "Epiphanes" outlined in Unit 37 and recapped in 38A. Before analyzing the contents of Daniel, additional comments about the nature of apocalyptic literature are offered in 38D.

The Apocrypha and Pseudepigrapha contain numerous apocalyptic writings, e.g., Enoch, Apocalypse of Baruch, etc. (see Unit 39). In pre-Christian times, these writings incorporated the following emphases:

1 **Dualism:** There are two forces at work in the universe and history. In the Old Testament, they are usually the God of Israel and any nation or foe opposed to Israel.

2 **Cosmic conflict:** The entire cosmos (earth, underworld, heaven, and their inhabitants) is involved in the struggle between good and evil.

3 **Eschatology:** This term refers to the events at the end of time, the last things. Apocalypticism concerns itself with two ages, the present and the future. It says that this present age is evil. Many inhabitants of earth are followers of the evil power. The righteous followers of God are helpless, oppressed, and persecuted. They may even be put to death by their evil contemporaries. Life in this present evil age is challenging. Things may get worse.

4 **Divine deliverance:** The only hope the righteous have is that God will intervene with power to deliver them. They are assured that God will soon engage their enemies in a cosmic conflict and overthrow them. After achieving this victory, God will usher in a new age that will be completely under His control. As a reward for their faithfulness, God's righteous followers will live under His divine protection and enjoy an eternity of blessedness.

5 **New age:** Although apocalyptic is pessimistic about the present age, it is optimistic about the eventual outcome. Within the present evil age, God's people are to remain faithful to God—no matter what. The day will come when the faithful will be vindicated. In some apocalyptic writings, the present evil world and age will be replaced by a newly created and incorrupt earth, or by a perfect heavenly city that will descend from above.

6 **Visions:** Apocalyptic literature often, but not always, makes use of visions in presenting its message. The visions serve as a literary device to gain attention and authority, and to provide an audience with "insider information."

7 **Pseudonymity:** The writings claim to be ancient, from the pen of some well-known figure. This gains them credibility and authority.

8 **Messianic figure:** While some apocalyptic writings refer to a coming messianic figure, Daniel and Isaiah 24–27 do not.

9 **Interim age:** Some apocalyptic writings refer to an interim period between the *end time* and the *new age*.

10 **Angels and demons:** Frequent mention is made of angels, both good and bad.

11 **Bizarre symbolism:** These writings make use of literary impressionism, such as references to mythological and astrological beasts and birds, to produce the desired effect.

12 **Numbers:** The ancients thought numbers had a mystical significance. Writers of apocalyptic literature show a developed interest in them.

13 **Coming woes:** As the end draws near, earthly disasters and irregularities in the heavenly bodies will occur. Even more, what takes place on earth is determined by what happens among the heavenly bodies. Events in the two spheres are related.

14 **Divine responsibility:** Humanity is relieved of any responsibility for the improvement of the present age. Everything must be left to God. Righteousness consists of loyalty and devotion to God, to be demonstrated by national loyalty and proper worship rituals. Wickedness demonstrates itself in idolatry, in the persecution of the righteous, or in belonging to a people other than the people of God.

38E

Antioch

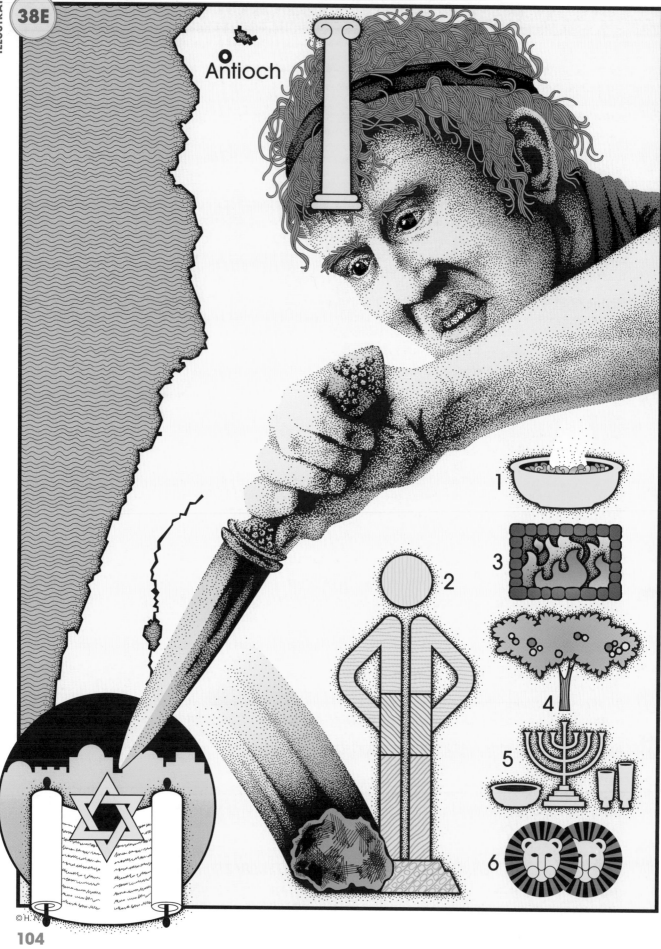

1

2

3

4

5

6

© H. N.

Daniel 1-6: The Stories

The Situation

1 Antiochus "Epiphanes" (*face, top right*) set out to destroy Judaism (*dagger directed toward Judah and Jerusalem*) and to force all Jews to embrace Greek *Hellenism* (*column*). He declared the *Torah* (*scroll*) to be invalid. His capital city was Syrian **Antioch**.

2 Antiochus placed an altar to Olympian Zeus in the outer court of the *Jerusalem Temple* (*Jerusalem skyline*) and sacrificed a pig on it. He erected an image of Olympian Zeus there also, and commanded the Jews to revere it. He threatened death to Jews who circumcised their male offspring. He forbade the Jews to worship according to the traditions of their fathers. He insisted that his subjects revere him as the incarnation of the deity ("Epiphanes," manifestation). He strove to expand the borders of his realm to what they had been when the Seleucids first came to power after the death of Alexander the Great. He robbed the Temple of its treasures and sacred vessels to help fund his campaigns.

3 The Book of Daniel is designed to make commentary on the situation described above, even though the setting for its contents is ostensibly the time of the Babylonian exile.

The Message

(Points 1–6 relate to Daniel 1–6, and to the details in the *lower right* of **ILLUSTRATION 38E**.)

1 *Bowl of food:* Daniel and his three friends (Hananiah, Mishael, and Azariah) are among those taken into captivity in Babylon by Nebuchadnezzar. All are given Babylonian names as a sign of their adoption by the king, 1:7. While undergoing a three-year training program to equip them to serve at the royal court in Babylon, they are to eat the food and drink the wine that the king provides for them, 1:5. They refuse to do so, and eat only traditional Jewish food for a trial period of ten days—at the end of which they prove to be ten times smarter than any of Nebuchadnezzar's magicians and enchanters, 1:8–21. (The food and drink Nebuchadnezzar offered them would have been viewed as unclean, as it might have been first offered to idols or prepared over firewood taken from a sacred grove. Only raw vegetables and water were safe from this danger.)

The message: Antiochus tried to stamp out all distinctively Jewish practices. All Jews were required to eat pork to demonstrate their willingness to cooperate with him. The writer's appeal is, "Do not eat Antiochus' pork [the king's rich food]."

2 *Image made from a variety of materials:* Nebuchadnezzar of Babylon has a strange dream. He demands that his wise men describe the dream and interpret it—and threatens them with death if they fail to do so. They cannot do so, and plead for mercy. Daniel, however, describes and interprets the dream.

The dream: Nebuchadnezzar saw in his dream an idol whose **head** was made of *gold*, **upper torso** of *silver*, **lower torso** of *bronze*, **legs** of *iron*, and **feet** partly of *iron* and partly of *clay*. A **large stone** not cut by human hands then bursts in, hits the image at its base, and shatters it—after which it grows until it becomes a mountain that fills the world.

The interpretation: Daniel tells Nebuchadnezzar that after his empire (head of gold) fades there will come a succession of empires. Alliances forged between the last two empires, and propped up by marriages between them, will come to nought. Finally, a kingdom (the kingdom of God) will break in. It will supersede all previous empires and hold eternal sway over the whole world.

The message to Daniel's readers: The Jews have suffered long under the Babylonians (gold), Medes (silver), Persians (bronze), Greeks (iron), and Ptolemies and Seleucids (iron and clay). Although at present they suffer under Antiochus, the bad times are almost over! The Kingdom of God will soon break in, and the Jews will be given authority to rule the nations of the world.

3 **_Fiery furnace:_** Nebuchadnezzar sets up an idol of gold and commands all to worship it. Three young Jews—Shadrach, Meshach, and Abednego—refuse to worship the image, despite the threat of death if they refuse. They declare that they will remain true to their God, who, although He can deliver them, may not choose to do so. They are then thrown into a fiery furnace, yet emerge unscathed and triumphant.

The message: Do not pay homage to the image of Olympian Zeus!

4 **_Tree:_** In a dream, Nebuchadnezzar sees an enormous tree with many leaves and bearing an abundance of fruit. Animals find shelter under it, and birds rest on its branches. A divine command is given to cut the tree down. Daniel tells Nebuchadnezzar that the tree represents him, and that he is guilty of great pride because he boasts about ruling the world. Although he will soon be cut down to size and afflicted with a form of madness that will cause him to behave like an animal, he will eventually be restored to sanity.

The message: Antiochus dreams of acquiring and controlling a vast realm. However, he is mad and God will soon cut him down to size!

5 **_Temple vessels:_** Belshazzar holds a huge banquet for the important people in his realm. In hosting it, he makes use of the vessels from the Jerusalem Temple that Nebuchadnezzar brought back to Babylon. During the course of the festivities, written words appear supernaturally on the wall of the palace banquet room: *Mene, mene, tekel, parsin.* Although these words represent weights, they may also be translated, "to number, to weigh, to divide"—signifying that God has counted Babylon's days, weighed the king in His scales and found him wanting, and divided up his realm. Babylon's end is near! That very night Darius the Mede destroys Babylon, and Belshazzar loses his life.

The message: Antiochus plundered the Jerusalem Temple, but God will not let him get away with it. God will soon destroy him and his realm.

6 **_Lions:_** Darius the Mede is manipulated into ordering his subjects to revere him as a divine being. Daniel refuses to do so, is thrown into a den of lions, but is miraculously delivered.

The message: Refuse to acknowledge Antiochus as divine in any way. God will soon deal with his arrogance.

The impression emerges that stories set in sixth century B.C. Babylon are addressed to much later situations. The historical veneer is transparent enough to reveal the real message readily to Jewish people who were experiencing that later history.

(The numbers below correspond to those in **ILLUSTRATION 38F**. When studying the contents of this section, note that Hosea 13:7,8 uses the terms *lion, bear,* and *leopard* as symbols of nations God said He would use to discipline His indifferent, rebellious people.)

Daniel sees the **four winds of heaven** (*top center*) stirring up the great sea, and a succession of four beasts rising out of the sea. The *great sea* represents the primordial ocean beneath the earth—referred to in Genesis 7:11 and 49:25. It was thought that various monsters dwelt within this sea—in particular, monsters that symbolized the chaos God overcame in ancient times, Job 26:13.

The four beasts represent the following empires and realms (*that match the numbers in the illustration*):

❶ Babylon (Daniel 7:4, **Babylonian ziggurat; winged lion**): In Babylonian art forms, Babylon was depicted as a winged lion. The two wings plucked out of the lion possibly represent Nebuchadnezzar and Belshazzar—both referred to in earlier chapters of Daniel.

❷ Media (Daniel 7:5, **head of a ruler of Media; bear with three ribs in its mouth**): The Medes, like all power-seeking empires, had destructive policies—hence the statement, "Arise, devour many bodies."

❸ Persia (Daniel 7:6, **winged leopard with crowned human head; four leopard heads, four wings**): Cyrus the Persian established his kingdom with the swiftness of an attacking leopard. The reference to the winged leopard having four heads signifies Cyrus and three of his successors (see 11:2).

❹ Greece (Daniel 7, **Greek helmet and sword; head of a dragon with ten horns; small horn** to right)**:** After Alexander the Great died in 323 B.C., his single kingdom became several kingdoms. Two opposing dynasties are referred to in the book of Daniel 9 (**two sets of horns**). The *Ptolemies* (named after Alexander's general, Ptolemy) ruled Egypt. The *Seleucids* (named after Alexander's general, Seleucus) ruled Mesopotamia (including Syria) and gained control of Judah in 198 B.C. Eventually, there appeared on the scene a Seleucid (Antiochus IV "Epiphanes", **little horn,** ❻) who sought control of Mesopotamia/Syria.

❺ In 175 B.C., Antiochus IV "Epiphanes" ❻ succeeded in gaining control of the **Seleucid Empire** (the **little horn** becomes a **big horn**). In doing so, he eliminated three other contenders (**three horns removed from dragon's head**). During his reign (175–163 B.C.), he sought to impose *Hellenism* (**Greek helmet and sword, and column**), Greek culture and religious beliefs, on all people living within his realm. In seeking to achieve this, he set out to destroy Jewish worship practices and religious beliefs (**sword pointing to Jerusalem Temple, priest's hat, five scrolls, and Star of David**).

❻ The number ❻ and the **horn** included in sections 4,5, and 7 relates to the person of Antiochus IV "Epiphanes," and his rise to power, ambitions, campaigns, and eventual fate. See 7:8,11,20,24–26; 8:23–25; 11:40–45.

❼ The grand finale to the vision in Daniel 7:1–8 is now described.

- **God** appears, seated on a **flaming throne with wheels**. The throne is surrounded by hosts of heavenly beings (**dotted circles around the throne**). See 7:9,10; Ezekiel 1.
- The dragon-like beast (*Greek Empire*) is destroyed, and Alexander's Seleucid successors (in particular— ❻ —Antiochus IV "Epiphanes," the "divine one"; the Jewish people referred to him as "Epimanes," the "mad one") are deprived of their dominion over the Holy Land (**arrow through the dragon's face and horns**). See 7:11,12.

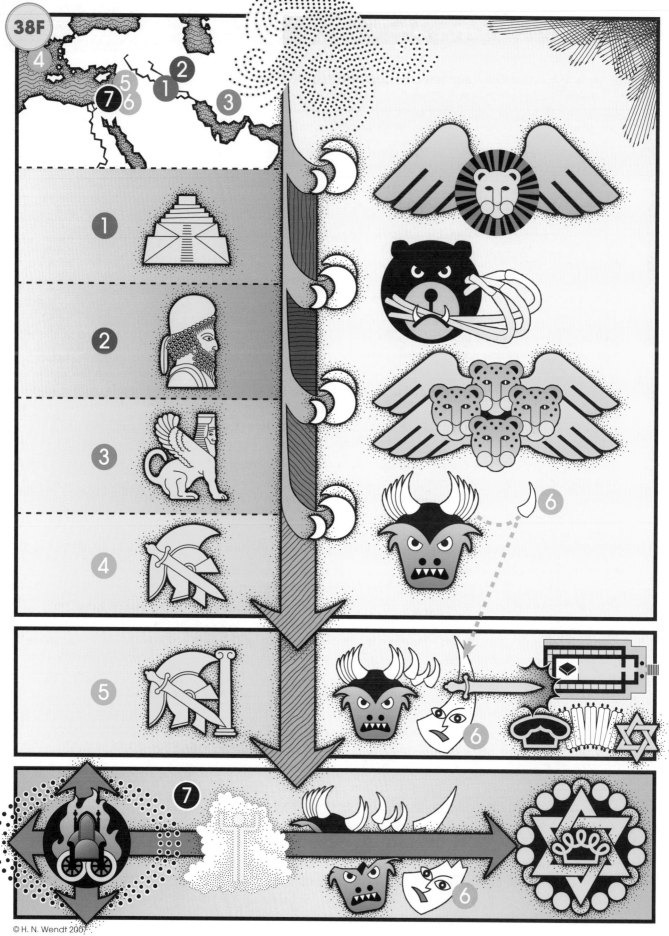

- *Cloud, male figure:* A heavenly "Son of Man" appears before God. See 7:13,14.

- *Arrow pointing to symbols of Judaism (crown, Star of David, circle of small circles):*
  In Daniel, the term "son of man" signifies the "holy ones," the "saints of the Most High," the
  Jewish people, 7:18. The vision encourages those facing death in Antiochus' persecution to
  stand firm. "God will not permit Antiochus' ravings to continue much longer. His Kingdom
  will soon break in. You, God's people, will constitute and rule it, and all nations will serve
  you forever!" (Read Daniel 7:15–27.)

  Prior to the breaking in of this final kingdom, the "saints of the Most High" will be delivered
  into the hands of the "little horn" for "a time, two times, and half a time," or three and a half
  years, 7:25. (A "time" signifies a year.)

Jesus applies the term "Son of Man" to Himself numerous times in relation to His servant ministry and
approaching crucifixion, Mark 8:31, 9:30–32, 10:32–34; Matthew 25:31–46. The use of the term "Son of Man"
in the Gospels denotes the fact that Jesus is the true Israel, Israel reduced to one. However, as the true
Israel, Jesus does not seek to *dominate* the world; He seeks to *serve* the world and to inspire His brothers and
sisters to do the same.

38G

 70 x 7

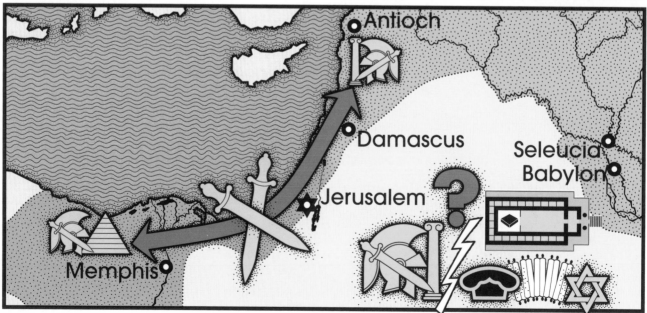

Antioch

Damascus

Seleucia
Babylon

Jerusalem

Memphis

Upper section

Daniel 8: Vision #2

1 *Verses 1–7:* A **ram with two horns** (*Perso-Median Empire*) is destroyed (**two horns, broken**) by a **he-goat with one horn** (Alexander the Great, *Greek Empire*).

2 *Verse 8:* After Alexander the Great's death (**one horn, broken**), his realm is divided up among four of his generals (**four horns**). Ptolemy and his successors rule Egypt (**pyramid, Greek helmet and sword**). Seleucus and his successors rule in Mesopotamia (**column, Greek helmet and sword**).

Verses 9–27: These verses focus on the efforts of Antiochus IV "Epiphanes" to destroy Judaism. Gabriel, the guardian angel of the Jewish people, now explains to Daniel what is taking place. A "little horn"— Antiochus IV "Epiphanes"—sprouts from one of the four horns, grows in size (**large horn**), and causes havoc. He interrupts the daily sacrifice in the Temple for 2,300 mornings and evenings, or 1,150 days, 8:14. Gabriel assures Daniel that the person and power of Antiochus will soon be broken, "by no human hand" but by God, 8:25.

The message: "Stand firm! God has things under control. God will soon bring Antiochus' blasphemous activities to an end and destroy him."

Middle section

Daniel 9: Vision #3

1 The angel Gabriel tells Daniel that the seventy years Jeremiah referred to when predicting how long the Babylonian exile would last really mean seventy weeks of years (**70 x 7**), or four hundred and ninety years (**490**); see Jeremiah 25:11, 29:10. The numbers referred to in the chapters should be understood, not in literal terms, but as "approximates."

Jeremiah's use of "seventy" signified that those taken into exile in Babylon in 597 and 587 B.C. would not return to the Promised Land within the immediate future. The existing generation of Jeremiah's day would pass away completely—and a new generation would make the journey from Babylon back to Jerusalem. But those who returned, and their successors, persisted in feeling that they had never really been rescued. They continued to live under a succession of foreign empires.

2 The angel Gabriel outlines the history of postexilic Israel in broad terms. Reference is made to an initial period of seven weeks (49 years), a further period of sixty-two weeks (434 years), and then a final week that is ushered in by the death of an "anointed one." During this final week, "the prince who is to come" will prevent the regular sacrifices from being offered for three and a half years. Then the decreed fate will overtake him.

The "anointed prince" referred to in 9:25 is either Cyrus (Isaiah 45:1), or the High Priest Joshua who presided over the rebuilding of the altar of sacrifice after the Babylonian exile, Ezra 3:2. The "anointed one" referred to in 9:26 was most likely the High Priest Onias III, who was murdered in 171 B.C. The writer links the beginning of the persecution by Antiochus IV "Epiphanes" to the time of Onias' murder.

The final "week" mentioned in 9:27 refers to the total period of the persecution by Antiochus IV "Epiphanes". Many Jewish people sided with Antiochus, and were happy to embrace the ways of Hellenism.

The reference to "half of the week," or three and a half days, refers to the length of Antiochus' final massive effort to do away with Judaism—which lasted for three and a half years.

Lower section

Daniel 10–12: Vision #4

The message of chs. 10–12 is similar to those in chs. 7 and 8. Ch. 10 is a prologue to the vision outlined in ch. 11, and ch. 12 is an epilogue.

1 A heavenly being, possibly Gabriel, appears to Daniel to give him a message. His coming was delayed by the patron angel of Persia (10:13), and he must soon return to face the patron angel of Greece, 10:20,21. The angelic visitor outlines to Daniel the history of surrounding nations as it relates to the history of the Jews. He refers briefly to the rise and fall of the Persian and Greek empires, concluding with comments about the division of the Greek empire after Alexander's death, 11:2–4.

2 Daniel 11:5–19 describes the parallel histories of the Ptolemies (***Greek helmet and sword, pyramid***) and Seleucids (***Greek helmet and sword, column***), including:

- Their campaigns against one another;
- Their alliances;
- Their intermarriage;
- Their intrigues;
- Their attempts to build empires for themselves.

Finally, Antiochus IV "Epiphanes" appears on the scene, 11:21. As part of his plan to impose *Hellenism* on all within his realm, he sets out to destroy *Judaism* (***Greek helmet and sword, column; fragmentation symbol; Jerusalem Temple, priest's hat, 5 scrolls, and Star of David,*** lower *right*). He deposes the High Priest, Onias III, and appoints Jason in his place, plunders Judea, invades Egypt, and robs the Jerusalem Temple during his return journey, 11:22–28. The Romans force him to terminate a second campaign against Egypt, 11:29–31. He attempts to seduce many Jews into embracing Hellenism, desecrates the Temple, and is opposed by the Maccabees, 11:33–35. He forsakes the gods his fathers worshipped, embraces the worship of Olympian Zeus, and claims himself to be divine, 11:36–39.

Predictions follow which suggest that Ptolemy will provoke Antiochus to invade Egypt again, unfortunately for the Egyptians, so successfully that Antiochus will conquer Libya and Ethiopia as well. However, during his return journey he will die somewhere between Jerusalem and the Mediterranean Sea, 11:40–45. These predictions were not fulfilled, and Antiochus died in the eastern region of his realm in 162 B.C.

3 Ch. 12 states that although a most difficult time lies ahead for the Jews, it will be of short duration and will be followed by a resurrection that will usher in the Kingdom of God, 12:1. Those whom Antiochus put to death will not miss out on this coming New Age; they will be raised from the dead to participate in it. On the other hand, those who were disloyal to the covenant and embraced Hellenism will rise to face judgment, 12:2,3. Indeed, the time of deliverance constantly draws closer, 12:5–13.

Scholars have been long aware that some of the details in Daniel pose historical problems.

1 Daniel 1:1 says that Nebuchadnezzar set siege to Jerusalem in the third year of Jehoiakim's rule, namely 606 B.C. However, Nebuchadnezzar became king only in 605 B.C., and set siege to Jerusalem in 598 B.C., Jehoiakim's eleventh year. Furthermore, Jehoiakim died before the city fell in 597 B.C. His son, Jehoiachin, succeeded him and was taken captive to Babylon, 2 Kings 24:12.

2 Nebuchadnezzar is said to have deported four *young* Judeans and commanded that they be trained in Babylonian wisdom for *three* years, 1:5. However, ch. 2 says that Daniel was already hard at work in the *second* year of Nebuchadnezzar's reign, and was made ruler over the province of Babylon after only *one* year of education in Babylon, 2:48. It is very unlikely that Nebuchadnezzar would have made a *youthful* Daniel ruler over Babylon.

3 Daniel 4 reports that Nebuchadnezzar went mad and was banished from Babylon for seven years. There are no other reports of this event. It would have been remarkable for a ruler such as Nebuchadnezzar in a land such as Babylonia to have resumed ruling after being out of control of his realm for seven years because of insanity. It is possible that this particular narrative is based on events during the life of Nabonidus (see 5 below). Nabonidus left Babylon to reside for ten years in the remote town of Tema in Arabia, where he forsook the worship of Marduk (the chief god of Babylon) and worshiped another god—the moon god Sin. His actions infuriated the priests of Babylon!

The Dead Sea Scrolls contain a prayer attributed to Nabonidus, in which he refers to the fact that he suffered from an ulcer for seven years. After praying in vain to gods of gold, silver, bronze, iron, wood, and stone, he sought help from a Jewish exorcist—who cured him, and ordered him to write a prayer of thanksgiving to the true God, the God of Israel.

4 If Daniel was taken to Babylon in 606 B.C. (1:1,2) and was still alive and active in the third year of Cyrus (535 B.C., 10:1), seventy-one years have passed since he was first taken to Babylon. He has also maintained his authority during the rise and fall of three empires.

5 Daniel 5 states that Belshazzar was Nebuchadnezzar's son. Not so—he was the son of Nabonidus, the last of the Neo-Babylonian rulers. Nabonidus came to the throne as a result of a revolutionary uprising, and was not a blood relative of Nebuchadnezzar. The Neo-Babylonian rulers were Nabopolassar (626–605), Nebuchadnezzar (605–562), Amel-Marduk (562–559), Neriglissar (559–556), Labashi-Marduk (556), and finally Nabonidus (556–539).

Furthermore, Nabonidus was not a Chaldean (5:30), but a Babylonian. Belshazzar was a co-regent with his father and could not properly be called a king. Cyrus the Persian, not Darius the Mede, conquered the Babylonians in 539 B.C., 5:30.

6 The identity of Darius the Mede poses a special problem. The historical records speak of Darius I, Darius II, and Darius III, but they were Persians, not Medes, and came *after* Cyrus, not *before* him. Efforts to identify a person who might rightly be called Darius the Mede have failed to produce a satisfactory answer. It is unlikely that there was a Darius the Mede who followed Belshazzar and preceded Cyrus.

7 The succession of empires listed in Daniel poses a problem. Chs. 2 and 7 state that three successive empires will arise after that of the Babylonians. The third is that of Alexander the Great, and the one before it the Persian Empire. Daniel understands the one which followed the Babylonians to have been

a Median empire ruled by Darius the Mede. However, it is unlikely that Darius the Mede ever existed; the realm of the Medes was made part of the Medo-Persian empire at least sixteen years before Cyrus replaced Nabonidus as king in Babylonia.

8 Daniel 4:34–37 says that Nebuchadnezzar came to faith in Daniel's God, and 6:25–27 states that Darius issued a decree to all nations that all people were to fear Daniel's God as the living God. There is no record of these events anywhere else, which is strange in view of their importance. It is unlikely that rulers such as Nebuchadnezzar or a hypothetical Darius the Mede would have dared infuriate the Babylonian priests by elevating the God of Israel to a place of importance above that of the Babylonians gods.

9 Daniel 8:14 states that the cessation of the daily sacrifice would last 2,300 mornings and evenings (1,150 days). In 7:25, the estimate is 3½ years. In 9:27 it is half a week of years, which again is 3½ years. In 12:11, the period is 1,290 days, and in the next verse it is 1,335 days. These variations are hard to reconcile if they are to be understood as prophecies made four hundred years before the event prophesied. However, they make more sense if the author is writing a number of separate pieces from time to time in the midst of an unfolding situation, and if the event to which he refers remains fixed in time, but draws closer.

When Was Daniel Written?

Two possibilities emerge:

1 Daniel was written during the historical experiences outlined in the first chapters (i.e., sixth century B.C.), and someone living during the middle of the second century B.C. determined that the book should be made public.

If this is the case, it seems strange that the writer would have been uncertain about contemporary history, but well-informed about events that were to take place four hundred years later.

2 It was written in the second century B.C. under the guise of having been written about four hundred years earlier.

The historical allusions, the inclusion of Aramaic sections (2:4b–7:28), and the kind of Hebrew language used, support the latter position. Ezekiel 14:14,20 links Daniel with Noah and Job, implying that he was a figure of antiquity. Ezekiel's reference was written during the period 593–587 B.C. The issue at stake here is not one of the *inspiration* of the work, but *literary genre*, namely, pseudonymous apocalyptic.

1 *For its own time:* Antiochus' ambitions and campaigns posed a serious threat. Many Jews who opposed him had to pay for their stand with life itself. Although the writer urges his compatriots to demonstrate courage and loyalty, he says more. He insists that all history is under God's control and direction. God will permit the powers of evil to go so far, but no further. Daniel suggests that God has revealed to some the divine blueprint about future events, which enables them to know when God will bring Antiochus' ravings to an end. Those suffering persecution should stand firm against the insane Antiochus, remain true to the faith of their fathers, and face even death with courage and hope. A day of resurrection and judgment is coming. When it does, the wicked will receive their due reward, and the righteous will be raised to share in the Kingdom of God that is about to burst into human history.

2 *For today:* God is still in control of history. Life in fellowship with God does not guarantee security and ease. It guarantees only the opportunity to be faithful to that God who, in grace, makes people His eternal children. The faithful can expect opposition from those around them in the world, Matthew 5:10–12, 10:16–33. However, when the world does its worst to them, all is well; they always rank among the "blessed" and are most precious to God, Matthew 10:29. Nothing can separate God's people from His love and fellowship in time or eternity; see Romans 8:31–39.

The Question of Canonicity

1 The question of what books were finally to be included in the Old Testament and what books excluded (*canonicity*) was determined by the Jews through lengthy discussions held at Jamnia during the close of the first century A.D. They placed Daniel among *The Writings*, not *The Prophets*. The prophetic section was considered complete and closed as early as 200 B.C. The discussions at Jamnia adjudicated only on the still "open" third section, *The Writings*.

2 Still today, Jews divide the Old Testament into three groups, *The Law*, *The Prophets*, and *The Writings*.
- *The Law* consists of the first five books in the Old Testament.
- *The Prophets* consist of Joshua through 2 Kings and Isaiah through Malachi (Ruth, Lamentations and Daniel excluded).
- *The Writings* consist of the remaining Old Testament books.

3 The evidence is that the book of Daniel was not known or quoted before approximately 160 B.C., but was known and quoted after that time. Considerations of literary style and vocabulary indicate a later date of writing, rather than a sixth century B.C. time frame.

38A After Alexander the Great succeeded his father Philip as ruler of Greece in 336 B.C., he devoted ten years (333–323 B.C.) to establishing an empire that extended from Greece to India to Egypt. After his death in 323 B.C. in Babylon, his generals fought for control of the realm. Eventually Ptolemy gained control of Egypt, and Seleucus gained control of Mesopotamia. Ptolemy and Seleucus and their descendants engaged in many battles—until the Romans assumed control of all their territories. There came the day when the Seleucid, Antiochus IV "Epiphanes," sought to eliminate Judaism and replace it with Greek culture and worship forms.

38B To understand the style and message of the book of Daniel, it is essential to know something about the difference between prophetic and apocalyptic writings. The foundation of the prophetic writings is the covenant God made with His people at Mt. Sinai; the problem is the spiritual indifference of God's people. Apocalyptic writings address situations in which God's people suffer under a foreign power—and the message is, "Stand firm! Trust God! He will deliver you soon!" Those who wrote apocalyptic literature did so under a pen-name at a time when the nation and they themselves were in danger. Because it was essential that the writer keep his identity a secret, he pretended to be a well-known ancient figure writing predictively about a deliverance that was soon to take place.

38C Down through the centuries, people have continued to write under a pen-name—not merely to conceal their true identity, but also to speak meaningfully to fellow-citizens facing threats.

38D The Apocryphal and Pseudepigraphical writings (see Unit 39) contain numerous apocalyptic writings. They speak to situations in which there are two forces at work in creation and history—the God of Israel and the foes of Israel. The message is usually that God will soon overthrow His people's enemies and lead His people into the New and Final Age.

38E The book of Daniel was produced by an anonymous Jewish writer during the time when Antiochus IV "Epiphanes" sought to abolish the Jewish faith in Judah and replace it with Hellenism. Although the author is unknown, he pretended to be a well-known Jewish personality living during the time of the Babylonian exile. Chs. 1–6 tell ancient stories linked to Babylonian, Median, and Persian control to speak to events taking place during the reign of Antiochus IV "Epiphanes."

38F In ch. 7, "Daniel" offers an outline of history from the Babylonian period to about 168 B.C., and continues with a prophetic account that covers the next three years. The literary device used gave his message an authority it would not otherwise have had. The message is that although God's people have suffered under the Babylonians, Medes, Persians, Greeks, and Seleucids, the day is coming when they themselves will rule the nations of the world—forever.

38G Ch. 8 describes the Greek empire destroying the Persian Empire, and gaining control of the Mediterranean world. Ch. 9 states that when Jeremiah predicted that God's people would remain in exile in Babylon for 70 years, he really meant 70 times 7–490 years. Although God's people were not really rescued from foreign domination in 538 B.C., things are about to change. They will soon be rescued from foreign domination once and for all—and they themselves will soon rule the nations of the world *forever*. Chs. 10–12 speak of the struggles between the Ptolemies and Seleucids, and the rise to power of Antiochus IV "Epiphanes." Ch. 12 assures those who lose their lives in opposing Antiochus will be restored to life and given a special place in the coming Messianic Age.

38H Although historical problems surface within Daniel, concern for historical accuracy takes second place to its message encouraging people to be faithful to God, no matter what the cost.

38I Daniel was given a place in the Hebrew scriptures toward the close of the first century A.D.—after Jesus' ministry. However, when Jesus spoke to the people of His day, He told them not to seek dominion over others in a brutal manner, but to devote life to serving others.

CROSS WAYS

4 SECTION

UNITS 31–40

The Postexilic Period and Judaism

UNIT 39
The Apocrypha and Pseudepigrapha

Jewish Writings 200 B.C.–A.D. 100

The concepts depicted are some of the central themes of the Jewish literature produced in the period between the Old and New Testaments. The numbers below correspond with those in **ILLUSTRATION 39A**.

1 *Star of David over Planet Earth:* The cherished hope is that the Kingdom of God will soon break in, and, when it does, the people of God (the Jewish people) will be given dominion over the nations of the world. Some hoped for the restoration of the Davidic dynasty in some form.

2 *Shattered Greek helmet, broken Greco-Roman column:* When the Kingdom of God breaks in, the cultures and military might of other nations and kingdoms will be shattered.

3 *Symbol for sin, question mark, cloud:* The postexilic community debated the question of the origin of sin. Many traced it back, not to the events described in Genesis 2 and 3, but to the events described in Genesis 6:1–4. Some argued that God created people with an evil disposition (*yetzer ha-rah*), but then gave them the Torah so that, through obedience to its law-codes, they could overcome evil and develop a good disposition (*yetzer ha-tov*) within themselves—and so make themselves acceptable to God.

4 *Angelic and demonic beings:* The writings produced during the intertestamental period contain numerous references to angels and demons, ascribing *names* to some of them and *differences in rank* among them.

5 *Scrolls; lamp* (*symbol for wisdom*)*:* The Old Testament contains a number of wisdom writings (see Unit 36); the Apocrypha contains two major wisdom writings: *Ecclesiasticus* (or *The Wisdom of Ben-Sirach*) and *The Wisdom of Solomon*. The Pentateuch (which, according to Judaism, God dictated to Moses at Mt. Sinai) was thought to be the supreme example of wisdom. Some personified Torah as Wisdom.

6 *Tombstone at ground level; two skull-filled realms below ground level:* The apocryphal and pseudepigraphical writings contain numerous references to life after death. After death, all go to Sheol, the abode of the dead, a shadowy underworld where all connections with God are cut off. Although some looked forward to the eventual resurrection of the body, not all shared this hope. As time went by, some taught that there were compartments in Sheol. The *righteous* would enjoy bliss while awaiting the day of resurrection, while the *wicked* would experience pain and agony.

7 *Cosmic signs of the times:* The breaking in of the New Age (the Kingdom of God, the Messianic Age) would be marked by cosmic signs within creation: *death throes*, indicating the end of the old order, and *birth pangs* heralding the new order. There would be cosmic upheavals, such as **huge waves, consuming fires, dark clouds, falling stars, changes in the color of the heavenly bodies**, etc. Creation itself would herald the breaking in of the New Age.

1 Although Malachi is placed last in the Protestant Old Testament, it was not the last book of the Old Testament to be written. Most likely Daniel was—in about 165 B.C. Hence, there is a gap of more than 200 years between Daniel and the first New Testament writing. Before and after Daniel was written, Jewish writings of all kinds were produced—history, wisdom, moral tales, poetry, apocalyptic. These writings are referred to as the *Apocrypha* and *Pseudepigrapha*. Although the writings of the Essene community at Qumran were also produced during this period, they are not included in the list of apocryphal and pseudepigraphical writings.

2 The term *Apocrypha* is derived from a Greek adjective meaning *hidden*. Some scholars suggest that originally the term signified *complementary*, and was applied to sacred books too exalted to be made available to the general public; see Daniel 12:9,10. Later the term was applied to books whose orthodoxy was questioned. By the fourth century A.D., the word *apocryphal* had become a technical term to describe the relationship of certain religious writings to those of the Old Testament Canon. It signified that, although these writings were edifying and had value for private study, they were not to be seen as inspired or used for reading in public worship.

3 The term *Pseudepigrapha* describes works that (*falsely*) claim to have been written by a famous ancient figure, such as Enoch or Baruch. Their contents are as varied as those within the Apocrypha, but they were seen to be on a lower plane and were viewed by some as heretical. They were not admitted into the TaNaK, or Old Testament canon, and no branch of the Christian Church sees them as having authority.

4 In *Protestant* Bibles, the Old Testament contains 39 books, the New Testament 27—a total of 66 books. Protestants define these 66 books as *canonical*, as having the right to a place in the *canon* of Scripture. *Canon* is derived from the Greek word *kanna*, which means a *reed* or *cane*. It came to mean a measuring instrument, and was first applied to the Bible about the middle of the fourth century A.D. when it denoted the list of *holy writings* that constitute the Bible. Later it became the name for the Scripture itself, indicating that it is vested with divine authority. When the term is used today, e.g., in *The Canon of the Old Testament*, it indicates that the Old Testament is a closed collection of writings inspired by the Holy Spirit that has divine authority, and is the rule for faith and life. When used in *The Canon of the New Testament*, the meaning is the same.

5 Bibles used by *Roman Catholics* and *Orthodox Christians* contain seven of the *apocryphal* writings: Tobit, Judith, 1 and 2 Maccabees, Wisdom, Ecclesiasticus (or Sirach), and Baruch, plus some additional passages in the books of Daniel and Esther. The Orthodox also include in their canon 1 and 2 Esdras, the Prayer of Manasseh, Psalm 151, and 3 Maccabees. The Roman Catholic Church uses the term *Apocrypha* to refer to those books the Protestant Churches define as the *Pseudepigrapha*. The *Anglican* communion relegates the apocryphal books to the position of an appendix to the Old Testament, include them in the lectionary, and commends them for devotional use and edification. *Reformed* communions generally follow the more conservative policy of the Jerusalem rabbis and omit them from the Scriptures.

6 During the three centuries of the pre-Christian era, Jewish people made their way into many parts of the civilized world—as mercenaries, merchants, adventurers, and slaves. During the Greek period that developed beyond the time of Alexander the Great (336–323 B.C.), Alexandria in Egypt became the home of a Jewish community second in importance only to that in Jerusalem. Because many Jews living in Egypt were no longer familiar with the Hebrew language, it became necessary to translate the

Hebrew scriptures into Greek—a translation that was known as the *Septuagint*. Because the Greek-speaking Jews were free from the rigid control of Jerusalem's religious leaders, they felt free to add to their collection of sacred writings other works that impressed them as having religious value.

7 The closing scenes of the *Old Testament* narrative (in Protestant Bibles) take place in a troubled world in which *Persia* ruled the Ancient Near East. The events of the *New Testament* take place in a world in which *Roman* arms and *Roman* law ensured peace and protection for all its citizens. Although the seat of power in this empire was located in Rome, the Greek way of life permeated that capital city and the realm over which it ruled. The common language used throughout the empire was Greek—a circumstance that enabled the New Testament writers to produce works in a language that could be understood in all corners of the realm. Paul and the early missionaries founded the first Christian communities in cities built on the Greek pattern, with schools and universities, pagan temples, and market places. In these cities, people—stimulated by Greek philosophers—discussed the nature of goodness and the existence of God. The period between the Testaments was largely one of Greek supremacy, and the writings produced during this period reflect the influence of Greece on the thinking of the most exclusive of all its subject people—the Jews.

8 The process of determining which books should be included in the Jewish Old Testament was a gradual one. It continued for several centuries and came to an end only about 20 years after Jerusalem had been destroyed by the Romans in A.D. 70. Because the Jewish people were now uprooted and had no national home, it was important that they should know what constituted their sacred writings—especially since the new sect of Christianity claimed to be the inheritor of the faith and promises of the Old Testament. The rabbis who met at Jamnia in A.D. 90 to determine the final list found themselves challenged. The problem lay with those books that had been circulating as sacred writings since the time when the books of the Law and the Prophets had been officially recognized—in about 200 B.C. There were various tests to determine which books were to be included in the Jewish scriptures. If a book had established a position for itself by virtue of its own worth, its hold on the affections of the people, its value as a guide to life, and as a treasury of the knowledge of God, it earned a place for itself in the Old Testament. Several books remained on the "borderline" for some time: Esther, Ecclesiastes, and Song of Songs. Esther was eventually included because of its link to a popular Jewish festival, *Purim*. Because the wholly secular Song of Songs was read as an allegory and given religious significance, it was included in the sacred canon.

However, the rabbis saw fit to reject those later Greek writings that had been in circulation abroad but not in Jerusalem. Books thought to have been written after the time of Ezra, or that could not be attributed to notable characters such as David and Solomon, were relegated to the category of Apocrypha, i.e. "hidden" from use in public worship.

9 When the New Testament opens, the Temple is the life-blood of the Jewish people, and Jewish pilgrims from far and near, at home and abroad, make their way to the Temple to worship God in the place of His appointing. The High Priest, with the permission of the Roman governor, exercises supreme authority over the life of the people. The party of the Sadducees, comprising the privileged priesthood, supports the High Priest in an uneasy association with the more popular party of the Pharisees. The Pharisees often debate for long hours about little things, but are basically patriotic and genuinely devout.

10 The synagogues located throughout Palestine (and wherever ten Jewish men banded themselves together in any part of the world) were the mainspring of religious life. Within their walls, the scriptures were read and the word of God was preached and taught. The synagogue may have had its origin in the Babylonian exile, but it was at the time of the great migration (*diaspora*) in the Greek period—when twice as many Jews lived outside Palestine as inside—that its real development took place. Similarly, while the Sadducees probably derived their name from Zadok (the priest at the time of David and Solomon), and the Pharisees were the successors of the godly upholders of the Law referred to in the book of Malachi, it was in the intertestamental period that the distinction between Sadducees and Pharisees sharpened into the familiar pattern revealed in the Gospels. The Sadducees saw themselves as supporters of progressive and internationally minded Greek ways; the Pharisees saw themselves as defenders of traditional, conservative Jewish practices.

When we move from the Old Testament to the New, we encounter words and ideas that, although implied in the Old Testament, have not been fully developed: the Kingdom of God, the Son of Man, Satan, Paradise, Gehenna, angels and demons, and an expectation of a catastrophic end of the world. These concepts began to take shape in the writings of the intertestamental period. They reveal what the Jewish mind was focusing on just before Jesus the Messiah carried out His radical servant ministry, and reflect the religious spirit that prevailed in the world where the writers of the New Testament grew up.

While we should not overemphasize the importance of the Apocrypha, we should not disregard writings that the major part of Christendom regards as canonical or edifying. Although the apocryphal writings do not match the spiritual heights of the Old Testament scriptures, they serve as the historical knot that ties the two Testaments together and set the stage for the breaking in of the Messianic Age.

THE APOCRYPHA

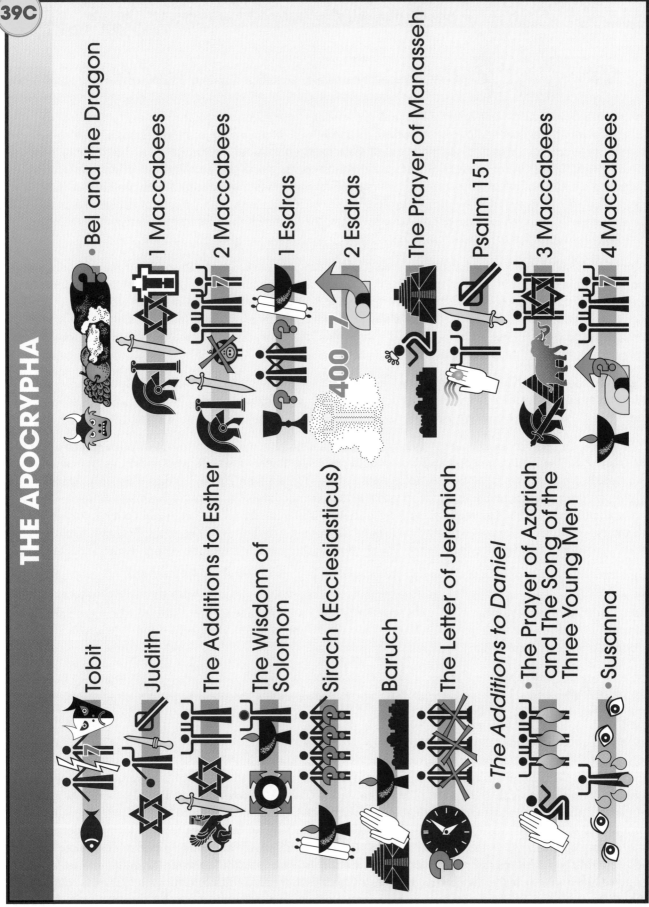

- Tobit
- Judith
- The Additions to Esther
- The Wisdom of Solomon
- Sirach (Ecclesiasticus)
- Baruch
- The Letter of Jeremiah
- *The Additions to Daniel*
  - The Prayer of Azariah and The Song of the Three Young Men
  - Susanna
  - Bel and the Dragon
- 1 Maccabees
- 2 Maccabees
- 1 Esdras
- 2 Esdras
- The Prayer of Manasseh
- Psalm 151
- 3 Maccabees
- 4 Maccabees

400

 **Tobit**

Tobit was a devout and wealthy Israelite who lived among those taken into exile in Nineveh (Assyria) in 721 B.C. Before being taken into exile, he worships and offers sacrifice only in Jerusalem and helps the widows, orphans, and proselytes living in Israel. He is married to Anna, an Israelite, who bears him a son, *Tobias* (**male figure**). After being taken into exile, Tobit refuses to eat the "unclean" Assyrian food. However, he attains a high position in the service of Shalmaneser, king of Assyria—during which time he deposits a large sum of money in far-off Media (to the southeast of today's Black Sea). After Sennacherib succeeds Shalmaneser, Tobit provides decent (but secret!) burial for those whom Sennacherib killed after returning from his attempt to destroy Jerusalem in 701 B.C.

When Tobit learns that Sennacherib knows what he is doing, he goes into hiding and then flees—and all of his property is confiscated. After Sennacherib is assassinated, his son and successor Esarhaddon permits Tobit to return to Nineveh, and restores to him his wife, son, and home. Some time later, after celebrating the Feast of Pentecost and burying an Israelite who had been murdered, Tobit loses his sight when bird droppings fall into his eyes. Although Tobit's wife works to support him, he finds his situation difficult to bear and prays for death to overtake him.

About the same time, *Sarah* (**female figure**), a young Hebrew woman in Ecbatana, prays for help. She is being haunted and tormented by the demon *Asmodaeus* (*demonic face*), who killed *seven of her suitors* (number "**7**") on their respective wedding nights. The angel Raphael sets out to heal them both.

Tobit sends his son Tobias to collect ten silver talents that had been left in Media. He hires a companion for his travels. We learn that the companion is actually the angel Raphael, who has taken on the human form of a certain Azariah. When the two travelers arrive at the Tigris River, Tobias catches a **fish**. On Azariah's advice, he preserves its heart, liver, and bile. They arrive in Ecbatana and stay at the home of Raguel, a kinsman of Tobit, who has a daughter named Sarah who is eligible for marriage. In due course, Tobias becomes betrothed to Sarah—who turns out to be his cousin. On their wedding night, Tobias burns the heart and liver of the fish he caught in the Tigris. The resulting smell drives the demon Asmodaeus to Egypt.

When Tobias returns to his father's home, he anoints Tobit's eyes with the gall of the fish—and his sight is restored. During a feast in Tobit's home, Azariah reveals that he is the angel Raphael and has been testing Tobit's faith and rewarding his virtue. Azariah then ascends into heaven. Tobit, Anna, Tobias, and Sarah live happily until the end of their days. The book closes after Tobit predicts the destruction of Nineveh and the rebuilding of Jerusalem.

 **Judith**

Judith was possibly composed during the time of the oppressive Antiochus IV "Epiphanes", the Seleucid ruler of Syria. It tells of Nebuchadnezzar (here called the ruler of *Assyria*, not *Babylon*) defeating the Medes, and then sending his general, Holofernes, to punish the local Israelites (**Star of David**) for refusing to support him. Holofernes lays siege to the town of Bethulia. Judith (**female figure**), one of the town's citizens and a beautiful and godly widow, is determined not to succumb to Holofernes' campaign. She prays fervently, puts on her brightest clothes, leaves Bethulia and makes her way to Holofernes' camp. After Holofernes welcomes her, she declares that she has military secrets to share with him, offers to help him defeat her people, and proposes that she stay in his camp until this is achieved. She uses her feminine charms to ensnare him and four nights later, while dining privately with a drunken Holofernes, she beheads him (**headless male figure, sword**). She then returns to Bethulia, **carrying the severed head** with her, and

the inhabitants greet her with great rejoicing. The Assyrians (who should have been Babylonians if Nebuchadnezzar was indeed their ruler!) discover the fate that has overtaken their leader, and when the citizens of Bethulia attack them, they withdraw. The people of Bethulia then give thanks to God.

The Additions to Esther

The Additions to Esther contains six passages designed to supplement *Esther* (***female figure***).

- The *first* (inserted before Esther 1:1) describes Mordecai (***male figure***), who was taken into exile in Babylon by Nebuchadnezzar, having a dream about coming events, and then warning King Artaxerxes of Persia (*winged leopard*) that two treacherous eunuchs, Gabatha and Tharra, are planning a conspiracy against him. After examining the eunuchs, Artaxerxes has them executed. Haman then plans to destroy Mordecai and the Jewish people because of what has been done to the two eunuchs.

- The *second* (inserted after 3:13) describes Artaxerxes, at the advice of Haman, drawing up an edict ordering the destruction of all Jews (***sword, star of David***) in his realm.

- The *third* (inserted after 4:17) contains the prayers of both Esther and Mordecai—prayers in which they pray to God to deliver them and the Jewish people from the threatened destruction.

- The *fourth* describes Esther meeting with the king so that she might persuade him not to carry out the decree.

- The *fifth* (inserted after 8:12) tells of the king issuing a decree annulling his former decree and permitting the Jews to defend themselves.

- The *sixth* (inserted after 10:3) reports Mordecai understanding the meaning of his initial dream. It adds a note describing how a letter about Purim was translated into Greek and taken to Egypt.

The Wisdom of Solomon

The author, who claims to be King Solomon, contemplates the nature of wisdom (***lamp***) in relation to religious faith and everyday life. According to many, the work constitutes the high point of Jewish wisdom literature. It encourages its readers to seek wisdom and lists the blessings that accrue to those who do. Wisdom is spoken of as a female celestial being (***female figure***), foremost among the creatures and servants of God (***symbol for God***). Its closing chapters review Old Testament history, and state that wisdom has helped the Jews but brought punishment and damnation to their opponents. Generally, the work encourages the Jews to hold fast to their faith. It makes use of Greek philosophical terms and speaks of the immortality of the soul rather than the resurrection of the body.

Sirach (Ecclesiasticus)

Sirach (*Ecclesiasticus*) consists of two large sections and a short appendix. It offers advice about how to live a successful life in the fullest sense.

- In the *first* section (chs. 1–43), it points out that the fear of the Lord and the keeping of the Law must go hand in hand. The writer sets forth much practical wisdom drawn from life experiences and urges that moderation be practiced in all aspects of life. Wisdom is revealed in the Law (*lamp, Torah scroll*).

● The *second* part of the work (chs. 44:1–51:12) analyzes the historical record of those who played a notable role in Israel's history (*four male figures, question marks*). Although it encourages praise for almost all of them, Solomon is referred to in a negative manner. This section ends with a hymn of thanksgiving.

 **Baruch**

Baruch, a work containing five chapters, presents itself as a work written in Babylon (*ziggurat*) by Jeremiah's friend and scribe.

● In the *first* section, the writer addresses the exiles and sets forth a confession of sins, a prayer for pardon, and a prayer for salvation (*praying hands*).

● In the *second* section, he praises Wisdom (*lamp*)—Wisdom being the content of the Law of Moses.

● In the *third* and final section, Jerusalem (*skyline*) laments over the exiles, but is then comforted and assured that the exiles will soon come back.

 **The Letter of Jeremiah**

The Letter of Jeremiah is usually included as the last chapter of Baruch, and purports to have been written by the prophet Jeremiah to the exiles in Babylon. The writer states that the Babylonian exile will be long, but not permanent (*clock face, question mark*). Idols (*three images*) and their accompanying evils and follies are exposed and ridiculed (*cancellation symbols*). They cannot tell right from wrong, or sanctify a vow or curse. The exiles are encouraged to shun these inanimate objects and not to worship or fear them.

• The Additions to Daniel

These consist of a number of short writings, some of which are appended to ch. 3 of the canonical book of Daniel.

 **• The Prayer of Azariah and The Song of the Three Young Men**

The Prayer of Azariah and *The Song of the Three Young Men* (appended to Daniel 3) contain what the title suggests: the prayer Azariah offered (*praying hands, kneeling figure*) in the fiery furnace, and the song of praise and repentance that the three young men sang as they walked about in the fire (*three male figures with raised hands, flames*).

 **• Susanna**

Susanna tells the story of the beautiful and righteous wife (*female figure*) of a rich Jew living in Babylon. Two lecherous Jewish elders (*four eyes*) are strongly attracted to her sexually and wish to have intercourse with her. One day they see her bathing (*drops of water*) and confront her with the choice of yielding to their sexual advances, or having them accuse her (falsely!) of being an adulteress. She chooses the latter. The people believe her accusers and condemn her. Daniel, a young, heroic figure, raises his voice in protest. A second trial is held with Daniel present. He questions Susanna's accusers, and reveals their testimonies to be contradictory. Susanna is justified and freed, and the elders are put to death.

• Bel and the Dragon

Bel and the Dragon ridicules idolatry. In the *first* story, King Cyrus is aghast at Daniel's scorn for the statue of Bel (***dragon's head***). He and the people in Babylon had been led to believe that each night the god Bel consumed the food (***fruit, bread***) of the sacrifices that the priests had set before him during the day. Daniel demonstrates that the priests, not the god, consumed the offerings—after sneaking into Bel's sanctuary each night through a secret door. The king has the idol destroyed and the priests executed.

A *second* story tells how Daniel, at the instigation of the mob, is thrown into a den of lions for refusing to revere a mighty dragon that was being worshiped in Babylon. However, Daniel is preserved for six days. On the sixth day, the prophet Habakkuk is supernaturally transported from Judea to where Daniel is imprisoned to supply him with food. Nebuchadnezzar releases Daniel on the seventh day and throws his accusers to the lions—who immediately devour them.

1 Maccabees

1 Maccabees outlines events from 175–134 B.C., namely the military campaigns (***sword***) led by Judas Maccabeus, Jonathan, and Simon against Antiochus IV "Epiphanes" who sought to destroy Judaism (***Star of David, Temple ground-plan***) and impose Hellenism (***Greek helmet, column***) on the Jewish people. (For additional details, see Units 37 and 38.)

2 Maccabees

2 Maccabees covers a period of history similar to that of 1 Maccabees, but focuses on the traumas of facing martyrdom during that period when Antiochus IV "Epiphanes" sought to impose Hellenism (***Greek helmet, column, sword***) on the Jewish people , 6:18–7:42. It describes Eleazar (***male figure***), and a woman and her seven sons (***female figure, male figure with "7" superimposed***) being put to death for refusing to eat pork (***pig, cancellation symbol***). The book's central theme is the eternal sanctity of the Jerusalem Temple and the faith of Judaism. The book makes a significant reference to the resurrection of the dead, 12:43–45.

1 Esdras

1 Esdras is a parallel account to the events recorded in 2 Chronicles 25–36, Ezra, and Nehemiah 7–8. It contains a large addition known as *The Debate of the Three Youths*, which tells of a contest among three Jewish guards at the Persian court of Darius. The contest consisted of a debate about the question, "Which is the strongest: wine, women, or truth?" (***wine chalice; female figures; Torah scroll, lamp***). The winner was Zerubbabel, who used the occasion to remind Darius of his obligation to allow the Jerusalem Temple to be rebuilt as quickly as possible. Zerubbabel's prize for winning the contest was permission to lead the Jews back to Jerusalem.

2 Esdras

The first two chapters are a Christian apocalypse thought to have been written some time after the fall of Jerusalem in A.D. 70. In them, God speaks to Ezra and reproves the Jewish people for their past unfaithfulness; God will reject Israel and turn to the Gentiles.

Chs. 3–12, and 13,14 are Jewish writings produced about A.D. 100. These 12 chapters are called *The Apocalypse of Ezra*, and consist of *seven* (**7**) visions. Among other things, the visions probe the end-times and questions relating to life after death (**open tomb, rising arrow**).

Apocalyptic writings such as *2 Esdras* express the hope that God will restore a fallen world in spite of the corruptions that prevail within it. They look forward to the creation of a new heaven and a new earth, in which there will be a new Eden and social harmony and fulfilment. In the biblical materials, the breaking in of the New Age is described as a process of an instant ("in the twinkling of an eye," 1 Corinthians 15:52), or 40, or **400** (2 Esdras 7:28), or 1,000 years (Revelation 20:2,7)—with or without a messianic ruler.

- In the *first* vision, (3:1–5:19) the seer asks why Zion has to suffer. After all, its sin is not as great as that of those who have been oppressing it. He is told that, although there is no satisfactory answer to his question, the new era will soon come. It will bring salvation and restore justice.

- The *second* vision (5:20–6:34) asks why Israel has been handed over to other nations. The seer is told that the age to come will soon break in. It will be a time of conversion and salvation.

- In the *third* vision (6:35–9:25), the seer asks why the Jews do not possess the earth. He is told they will do so in the coming messianic age. Details are revealed about the coming judgment, messianic age and afterlife, and the question about whether the number of the elect is limited.

- The *fourth* vision (9:26–10:59) describes a woman (Jerusalem) deep in mourning. She lists her many woes and is then transformed into a glorious city.

- In the *fifth* vision (chs. 11,12) the writer sees an eagle (Rome) with twelve wings and three heads. Rome (not Greece) is seen to be the fourth beast mentioned in Daniel 7; the Messiah will rise up and replace it.

- The *sixth* vision (ch. 13) describes a man rising up from the sea and then riding on the clouds of heaven (male figure, cloud) to destroy a multitude of evildoers.

- The *seventh* vision (ch. 14) outlines how Ezra restored the sacred books of the Hebrews. He accomplished the task with help of a vision and five supernaturally inspired scribes. They produced not only the Hebrew scriptures but also seventy apocalyptic or esoteric works. Ezra is finally taken up into heaven.

The concluding section (chs. 15,16) is of Christian origin and deals with God's judgment of the nations and the tribulations at the end of history.

The Prayer of Manasseh

The Prayer of Manasseh claims to be the prayer King Manasseh prayed (**crowned, praying male figure**) after being taken from Jerusalem (**skyline**) into exile in Babylon (**ziggurat**). Manasseh regrets his former apostasy and hopes for divine forgiveness. The prayer is referred to in 2 Chronicles 33:10–20.

Psalm 151

This is a psalm supposedly composed by David (*annointing hand, oil; male figure*) after he killed and beheaded Goliath (*headless figure, sword*). David extols himself as God's champion and the leader of a resurgent Israel.

3 Maccabees

The title is a misnomer. The events described in the book take place during the late third century B.C., forty years before the Maccabean revolt. It reports three incidents in the struggle between Ptolemy IV (221–203 B.C.) and the Jews.

- After defeating the Syrians at Raphia in 217 B.C., Ptolemy IV of Egypt (*Greek helmet, pyramid*) undertakes a tour of the temples in his domain. When, at the intercession of the High Priest Simon II, he is prevented from entering the Jerusalem Temple, he is enraged and orders a persecution of the Jews in Egypt (*sword; Star of David, two male figures in posture of praise*).

- Ptolemy insists that all citizens of Alexandria sacrifice to the Egyptian gods. The Jews who refuse are to lose their citizenship, be branded, and made slaves. Only a few Jews yield.

- Ptolemy gathers the Jews together up in the Hippodrome at Alexandria and lets loose among them 500 elephants (*elephant*) that have been maddened with wine. However, the elephants trample the Egyptians instead! The king repents, frees the Jews in his realm, gives them a feast, and sends them home.

4 Maccabees

4 Maccabees is a religious discourse on the supremacy of wisdom and reason (*lamp*). Obedience to the Jewish Law represents the triumph of spirit over bodily sensations and human passions. It tells stories from the Old Testament and Jewish history to support its message: e.g., Joseph resisted the temptations of Potiphar's wife; Moses overcame anger, etc. Martyrdoms recounted in 2 Maccabees— Eleazar (*male figure*), and a woman and her seven sons (*female figure, male figure with "7" superimposed*) being put to death for refusing to eat pork—are held up as an example of how unwavering faith leads to salvation. When dealing with the issue of life after death (*open tomb, rising arrow, question mark*), the writer focuses on the immortality of the soul rather than on the resurrection of the body.

THE PSEUDEPIGRAPHA

• *Baruch Literature*

• 2 Baruch

• 3 Baruch

The Psalms of Solomon

The Sibylline Oracles

The Testament of Moses

• *Enoch Literature*

• 1 Enoch

7,000 + 1,000

• 2 Enoch

• 3 Enoch

49x49

The Book of Jubilees

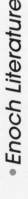

x12

The Testaments of the Twelve Patriarchs

αβχ
6x12

The Letter of Aristeas

• The Enoch Literature

Genesis 5:24 states, "Enoch walked with God, and he was not, for God took him." Because Enoch supposedly went directly to heaven, many legends were produced about him. Three books bear his name.

• 1 Enoch

1 Enoch is the book usually meant when *Enoch* is referred to. It is a *collection of literature* consisting of five sections.

- In the *first* section (1–36), a final judgment is predicted. Enoch is told that humanity has been corrupted by fallen angels. These fallen angels are doomed. Enoch is taken on a guided tour of another world where he sees Sheol and the Garden of Righteousness.

- In the *second* section (37–71), the parables about the Son of Man that were revealed to Enoch are listed. Here "parable" refers to a certain kind of discourse that makes use of a vision, a prophecy, or a poem. The first parable deals with the coming judgment and reveals some astronomical secrets. The second deals with the Head of Days and the Son of Man, the Elect One; see also Daniel 7:9,13. The third depicts the blessedness of the saints and judgment by the Elect One.

- Section *three* deals with astronomical matters. It describes the disorder that will take place among the heavenly bodies prior to the final judgment.

- Section *four* contains two dream visions. The first speaks of the deluge that is about to come to punish the world. The second deals with the history of the world from creation to the "end time" in which the author is living. It is in the form of an animal allegory and refers to the Messiah (who appears in the guise of an animal) and the New Jerusalem.

- The *fifth* section contains Enoch's admonitions, an apocalypse of weeks, and references to the Messiah and the birth of Noah.

The book of *Enoch* contains some significant teachings. It describes the future life in terms of earthly pleasure and says that marriage and family life will be part of the scene (***heavenly cloud, parents, children***); note Mark 12:18–27. Sheol is no longer just a place to which all the dead go, but a place where the wicked are punished (***flames, male and female figures***). The book contains numerous references to angels and ascribes names to them. The fallen angels referred to in the *first* section were those who sinned with women (***winged creature, female figure, fragmentation symbol***); see Genesis 6:1–4. They introduced women to such evils as weapons, cosmetics, and enchantments. The offspring of these evil unions were destroyed by the flood, but their spirits still roam about the earth and cause much evil. The wicked angels are subject to one particular demon, Satan. However, more than one angel acts as a *satan* or *adversary*.

Enoch contains references to a figure called the *Son of Man*. He is pictured as a heavenly figure who accompanies God. His task is to support the righteous and be a light to the Gentiles. He is filled with the spirit of wisdom and understanding. He will carry out the final judgment, destroy the wicked, and rule over all. The righteous will be saved and participate in an eternal banquet with him.

7,000+1,000 • 2 Enoch

Second Enoch contains interesting references to a millennium. It states that the history of ***Planet Earth*** will last ***7,000*** years, and that the 8th period will be a ***1,000*** year millennium.

• 3 Enoch

3 Enoch is a mystical apocalypse. Genesis 5:24 suggests that Enoch was spared physical death and taken directly into heaven (***Planet Earth, rising figure, seven levels in the heavenly realm***) where, according to later rabbis, he witnessed and experienced divine revelation. Some believed that Enoch and Moses would reappear when the messianic age broke in.

The Book of Jubilees

The Book of Jubilees is also known as *Little Genesis* or as *The Apocalypse of Moses*. The work shows great interest in calendric matters. It divides the history of the world from creation to Sinai into **49** periods of **49** years. (A *jubilee* is 49 years.) It opposes attempts to foster Hellenism by emphasizing the importance of proper Sabbath observance (***approval sign on "7"***), dietary laws (***food, approval sign***), and circumcision. It attacks idolatry (***idol; cancellation symbol***) and nudity as practiced in Greek athletic contests (***running nude male figure, cancellation symbol***). It says much about brotherly love, but the reference is to Judaism exclusively. Contact with impure Gentiles is to be avoided. These concerns date from the Maccabean period.

Jubilees contains only one reference to a messianic figure, a prince descended from Judah. It concerns itself more with salvation through the observance of the Law. The Law is eternal and written on heavenly tablets. Even the angels have been under obligation to observe the Sabbath and practice circumcision since creation. The Law is perfect truth. Revelation consists in making this Law known to humanity. However, some of the laws listed in *Jubilees* differ from, and are more stringent than, those in the Pentateuch.

The book does not display the developed interest in angels that *Enoch* does. Although it ascribes no names to angels, it distinguishes several classes of them, including an inferior class set over the forces of nature. Like *Enoch*, it says that the evil angels fornicated with women, and traces the fall into sin to that event. It focuses, not on the resurrection of the body, but on the immortality of the soul.

The Testaments of the Twelve Patriarchs

The Testaments of the Twelve Patriarchs employs a form well-known in Judaism in which a famous figure delivers a speech just before his death. In it, he shares parting advice and admonitions with his children or followers. As Jacob (***reclining figure***) gave a blessing to each of his ***twelve sons*** (Genesis 49), so The Testaments speak of each of Jacob's twelve sons giving a parting blessing to his own sons. Each follows a set pattern:

- The patriarch is described and his age given.
- Details are given about the patriarch's life, trials, and visions.
- The patriarch's listeners are encouraged to avoid evil and to seek virtue.

- The hearers are instructed about the future, e.g., to obey Levi and Judah. Reference is made to the coming of the High Priest and the Messiah.
- Each presentation concludes with information about the patriarch's death.

Some of the contents appear to be Christian additions. In places, the work supports the expectation of two Messiahs, one an anointed High Priest from the tribe of Levi (**priest's hat**), and the other an anointed king (**crown**) from the tribe of Judah. The Qumran Community, from which the Dead Sea Scrolls come, shared a similar expectation. *The Testaments* contains a developed demonology. Beliar is the leader of the forces of evil (**demonic faces**). Eventually, the High Priest from Levi will overcome him and cast him into the eternal fire (**flames**); see 2 Corinthians 6:15. In the resurrection, the righteous will reside in the New Jerusalem. Whether this will be on earth or in heaven is not stated.

The Letter of Aristeas

This small book claims to have been written by Aristeas to his brother Philocrates—to provide him with information about the origins of the Greek translation of the Pentateuch. The story is as follows:

A well-known statesman, Demetrius of Phaleron, was the librarian for Ptolemy II Philadelphus. He felt the need to obtain copies of the Hebrew Torah (**five scrolls**) for the famous library in Alexandria. At his urging, Ptolemy requested these from the High Priest in Jerusalem. The High Priest responded by sending to Egypt a band of seventy-two translators, **6** from each of the **12** tribes. They completed the required translation from Hebrew into Greek (**three Greek letters**) to the satisfaction of all concerned. (The term Septuagint, which means "seventy," now applies to all of the Greek Old Testament, not just to the Pentateuch.)

• Baruch Literature

In addition to the apocryphal book of Baruch, several pseudepigraphical books are ascribed to him, and two are seen to be very important.

• 2 Baruch

2 Baruch (also known as *The Syriac Apocalypse of Baruch*) depicts visions experienced by Baruch after the fall of Jerusalem (**damaged walls**). The visions explain that tragedy and the ensuing Jewish suffering. It contains visions of the last times, the Messianic banquet (**food, chalice**), and the resurrection of the dead (**open tomb, rising arrow**).

• 3 Baruch

3 Baruch (also known as *The Greek Apocalypse of Baruch*) describes an angel taking Baruch to the level of the "**fifth heaven**" (11:1; see also 2 Corinthians 12:2) and showing him numerous heavenly images. The writing displays a developed interest in the roles of **angels** as guardians and mediators.

 **The Psalms of Solomon**

The Psalms of Solomon consist of eighteen psalms composed by Jews in Palestine in the first century B.C. It is possible to date some of their historical references—for example, Pompey's siege of Jerusalem in 63 B.C., 8:15–21. Psalms interprets this invasion as God's punishment of Israel for the worldliness of its rulers—at that time, the Hasmoneans. It opposes the Sadducean priestly rulers (***priest's hat and crown cancelled out***), as do the writings of the Qumran Essenes.

The work expounds a theology of free choice between God and evil, and speaks of divine retribution. Psalms 17 and 18 pray for the coming of an anointed (***annointing hand, oil***) Davidic Messiah who will bring the Gentile world under his yoke (***Star of David over Planet Earth***). The Messiah will be a sinless man who will renew Jerusalem (***skyline***) and establish Israel as God's kingdom. Jesus consistently rejected such expectations.

 **The Sibylline Oracles**

About 500 B.C., Heraclitus of Ephesus referred to Sibyl, a prophetess of Cumae. Later in the Hellenistic world certain (usually old) women were thought to have been filled with the divine spirit and equipped to act as channels through whom the gods could deliver their oracles to humanity (***female figure, throne-like seat***). At least ten such women ("Sibyls") were honored at various shrines. Both Jews and Christians imitated the pagan practice and composed *sibylline oracles* of their own. Most of these oracles have been lost, but some have survived. In these, the future course of world history is described. Beliar will be destroyed (***satanic face, cancellation symbol***), the Jews (***Star of David***) will ultimately triumph, and the Messiah, the Anointed One (***annointing hand, oil***), will come. Noah's daughter is the *sibyl* who speaks in them. Many of these oracles served as Jewish propaganda.

 **The Testament of Moses**

Some biblical scholars believe that originally there were two works, *The Testament of Moses* and *The Assumption of Moses*. Some suggest that the two writings were combined at an early date, perhaps under the title of the *Assumption*. What survives is basically the *Testament* section of the combined work.

In this section, Moses, shortly before his death, speaks to Joshua and outlines the future history of Israel within the ***land of Canaan*** from the time of the conquest (***sword***) until the time of the Messianic Age (***annointing hand, oil***). The work is actually a pseudepigraphical "prediction," or summary in retrospect, from the author's own time (note the comments on Daniel in Unit 38). The historical details carry right through until the author's own time, 4 B.C.–A.D. 30 (including the Greek period, ***Greek helmet***) and express Judaism's eventual reaction to Roman domination. The writer expects the end to come soon and Judaism to be delivered from Roman oppression. Although God's kingdom will eventually be established, no reference is made to any Messiah figure in relation to this expectation. Ch. 9 describes Taxo, a Levite, exhorting his seven sons to accept martyrdom for the sake of their faith; see also 2 Maccabees 6 and 7.

The lost part of the book, *The Assumption of Moses*, apparently dealt with the death of Moses and his assumption (being "taken up") into heaven. His final assumption took place after a struggle for his body between the archangel Michael and Satan; see Jude 9. References to this book occur in the writings of the early church fathers.

39A In addition to the books of the Hebrew Scriptures and the Protestant Old Testament, other Jewish writings exist that date from the period 200 B.C.–A.D. 100. These works are referred to as the Apocrypha and Pseudepigrapha. Both collections give valuable insights into ideas and teachings that developed during the period 200 B.C.–A.D. 100. Some of the issues that surface within them are:

- The hope that the Jewish nation will eventually rule the world.
- The fate that will eventually overtake the culture and military might of other nations.
- The origin of sin.
- The existence and role or heavenly beings—both good and evil.
- The concept of wisdom.
- The cosmic signs that will precede the breaking in of the messianic age.
- The nature of life after death.

39B Although many Christian Bibles contain the Apocryphal writings, the number of writings included varies. Section 39C lists 18 Apocryphal books. The term "Apocrypha" is derived from a Greek word meaning "hidden"; it was eventually applied to those sacred books whose orthodoxy was questioned. Although it was conceded that these writings are edifying and have value for private study, they were not seen as inspired nor were they read in public worship. The Roman Catholic Church includes seven apocryphal writings in its canon, and refers to them as *deuterocanonical*. The Orthodox Church includes 12 apocryphal writings in its Old Testament canon.

The Pseudepigrapha is another collection of intertestamental writings. The name denotes that they are pseudonymous; their authorship is ascribed (falsely) to an ancient person. Although 13 of these writings are listed in section 39D, more are being added to the list. The Roman Catholic Church refers to these writings, and the three apocryphal books it denies a place among its deuterocanonical books, as the Apocrypha.

39C The Apocryphal writings vary in content and focus. Tobit, Judith, The Additions to Esther, The Additions to Daniel, Susanna, Bel and the Dragon, 1, 2, 3, and 4 Maccabees are narrative writings. The Wisdom of Solomon, Sirach, Baruch, and 1 Esdras focus on the concept of wisdom. The Letter of Jeremiah and 2 Esdras offer meaning and hope to God's suffering people. The Prayer of Manasseh is the prayer that a repentant King Manasseh is said to have prayed after being taken into exile in Babylon. Psalm 151 was supposedly prayed by David after he killed Goliath.

39D The contents of the Pseudepigraphical writings resemble those of the Apocryphal writings. Much of the Enoch literature focuses on "end-time" events. The Book of Jubilees divides the history of the world from creation to Sinai into 49 periods of 49 years; among other things, it attacks Greek and pagan practices. In The Testaments of the Twelve Patriarchs, Jacob's twelve sons give "farewell death-bed speeches" to their offspring. The Letter of Aristeas describes events having to do with the translation of the Hebrew scriptures into Greek. Second and 3rd Baruch contain numerous visions that have to do with the "end-time." The Psalms of Solomon explain why God permitted the Romans to invade Judah in 63 B.C., and define some messianic hopes. In The Sibylline Oracles, Noah's daughter provides information about what will take place in the end-time. In The Testament of Moses, "Moses" outlines the history of God's people from the time of the conquest until the breaking in of the Messianic Age. He also assures the Jewish people that they will eventually prevail over their Roman overlords.

CROSS WAYS

4
SECTION

UNITS 31–40

The Postexilic Period and Judaism

UNIT 40
Messianic Hopes

Messianic Expectations at the Time of Jesus

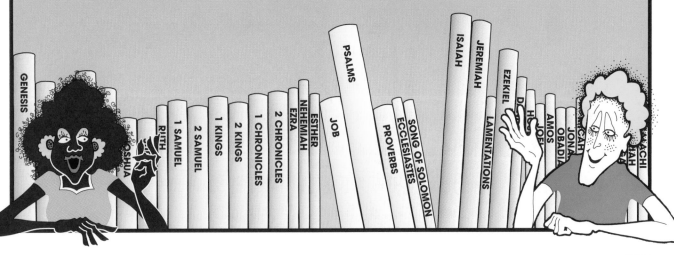

Nineveh

Ashur

721

597

587

538

Samaria

Jerusalem

582

Babylon

The Jewish people believed that God had entered into a unique relationship with them through His covenant with Abraham and the covenant He made with them at Sinai. They believed that the day would come when they would enter into the visible honor, glory, and supremacy over the nations which, as they saw it, was their right as God's covenant people. Many believed that the Messiah would be the agent through whom God would fulfill their destiny. During the postexilic period, a variety of hopes prevailed concerning the nature of the ministry the expected Messiah would carry out. **ILLUSTRATION 40A** depicts some of these hopes—and their historical background.

1 *Arrow to Nineveh and Ashur:* The Assyrians destroyed the Northern Kingdom of Israel in 721 B.C., and took many thousands of its leaders and citizens into exile.

2 *Two arrows to Babylon (ziggurat):* Nebuchadnezzar devastated Judah in 597 and again in 587 B.C., and took two of its kings (***two crowns***) and its leading citizens into exile on both occasions. In 587 B.C., Nebuchadnezzar destroyed Jerusalem and its ***Temple*** (*top left*).

3 *Arrow pointing to Egypt (pyramid)* serves as a reminder that many living in Judah fled to Egypt in *582* B.C. after some Judeans killed Gedaliah, the Jewish governor appointed by the Babylonians, and his Jewish and Babylonian associates, Jeremiah 41:1–43:7.

4 *Arrow from Babylon to Judea:* When Cyrus the Persian conquered the Babylonians in 539 B.C., he permitted national groups living in exile in Babylon to return to their homelands. The Judean exiles began returning in *538* B.C. Although many had hoped that King Jehoiachin (taken into exile in Babylon in 597 B.C. at the age of 18) would return and be reinstated as king in Jerusalem, he died in Babylon prior to the return (***crown, question mark, cancellation symbol***). The Davidic dynasty was no more!

5 What did the exiles hope to experience when they returned to Judah?

    a.   They hoped that they would return to a Messianic Age in a Judah that was a virtual new Garden of Eden, Isaiah 51:1–3. They would live in large homes (***house***, *lower left*) surrounded by large vineyards (***vine, grapes***) that would produce an abundance of wine.

    b.   The wealth—the gold and silver—of Gentile nations (***sack containing coins***, *lower left*) would flow into Judah and Jerusalem (***arrow from sack to Judah***), Zechariah 14:14, Isaiah 60:5; 61:6b. ***Ships*** and ***camels*** (*center left*) would bring this wealth to Judah across the seas and the deserts, Isaiah 60:5,6,9,11.

    c.   Those of God's people who had been scattered around the Mediterranean world and Mesopotamia would return to Judah, bringing their treasures with them, Isaiah 60:9.

    d.   The day was coming when the Gentiles would serve God's people! They would feed their flocks, and care for their crops and vines, Isaiah 61:5.

    e.   Some in Judah hoped that God would bring the nations who had caused them grief to Jerusalem and empower God's people to crush them as a person crushes grapes in a winepress, Joel 3:1–13. God would take vengeance on the Gentiles, Isaiah 61:2! Plagues and death would overtake those who attacked Jerusalem, Zechariah 14:12,13.

6 However, those who returned to Judah were *grief-stricken* (***faces***, *center right*) by what they found upon their return. What they found waiting for them in Judah was not a *dream-world Messianic Age*, but a *mess* (***rubble***, *bottom right*).

When Jesus preached His first sermon in His home town of Nazareth (Luke 4:16–30), He used Isaiah 60:1–61:6 as the basis for what He proclaimed (Unit 46). However, Jesus omitted those sections of the passage that pointed to vengeance, nationalism, prosperity, and power, added that Elijah and Elisha had both shown compassion to *Gentiles*—to the widow of Zarephath (a Phoenician) and Naaman the leper (a Syrian)—and then declared that in Him the Messianic Age had broken in. Jesus' hearers responded by plotting to throw Him off a cliff, Luke 4:28,29. (Note that the term "Christ" is a *title*, not a name; it means "the Anointed one," the Messiah. It is more appropriate to refer to Jesus as Jesus *the Messiah*.)

Messiah: Where, Who, and for Whom? 40B

 The Messianic Age

Center section

Jerusalem skyline: Jerusalem and its Temple would be the focal point for life in the Messianic Age, Isaiah 2:2–4; Micah 4:1–4. The Messiah would be enthroned in that glorious City of David, and all nations would honor him and the Jewish people.

Treetops touching above Jerusalem: The Holy Land would be as beautiful as was the Garden of Eden prior to humanity's fall into sin, Isaiah 51:1,2.

Lamb, lion, ox, and serpent: Animals would not maul each other, nor would they attack humans. Harmony would prevail among the nations, and God's people would live in peace, Isaiah 11:6–9.

Crops to right and left of Jerusalem: The soil would produce large grain crops and clusters of huge grapes to provide the people with vast quantities of wine, Amos 9:13; Joel 3:18.

 The Messianic Deliverer

Top left

The Messiah would be a ruler descended from David (***crown***), endowed with wisdom (***lamp***), whose rule would give rise to peace, harmony, and plenty among God's people, Isaiah 9:1–7; 11:1–5.

Top right

Symbol for God breaking in through the clouds: Some hoped that God Himself would descend from the heavens into human history to inaugurate the Messianic Age, Isaiah 64:1,2.

Lower left

Crown, halo, sword: A pseudepigraphical writing, Psalms of Solomon 17 and 18, points to the coming of a divinely endowed descendant of David who would destroy Israel's enemies and bestow upon the nation the blessings of the Messianic Age.

 Participants in the Messianic Age

Lower right

Question mark, Jewish person inside symbol for covenant, Gentile person outside symbol for covenant: Jewish teachers taught that *all Jews* would participate in the Messianic Age. Some Jewish sects insisted that only *righteous Jews* would be resurrected so that they might participate in the Messianic Age. But what role would the Gentiles play in that Age, and on what terms? Some believed that the Gentiles would take part in the Messianic Age *if they converted to Judaism.* Others believed that the Gentiles would not participate in it. Others again believed that the Jewish people would rule over the Gentile nations—who would become their servants and slaves.

In the sections that follow, additional insights are offered concerning the hopes and beliefs depicted in **ILLUSTRATION 40A** and **ILLUSTRATION 40B**.

A DAVIDIC DELIVERER

1 One line of Messianic hope grew out of the establishment of the Davidic dynasty and the expectation that it would last forever. Second Samuel 7 outlines how David proposed to build a "house" (temple) for God. However, God told David that *he* would not build a "house" (temple) for God, but that *God* would make a "house" (dynasty) out of David. At the same time, God promised David, "Your house and your kingdom shall be made sure forever before me; your throne shall be established forever," 2 Samuel 7:16. Prophet after prophet repeated this promise and interpreted the Messianic ideal in the light of it, Isaiah 11:1,10; Jeremiah 23:5; 30:9; 33:15,17,22; Ezekiel 34:23; 37:24; Hosea 3:5; Amos 9:11; Micah 5:2–4; Zechariah 12:8.

2 In its earliest form, hopes relating to the coming Davidic king were simple. There would be prosperity, freedom, security, justice, and goodness under a kind, righteous king who would rule with wisdom and power. (In certain passages in Isaiah, this dream appears at its loveliest, Isaiah 4:2–6; 9:2–7; 11:1–9.) The coming descendant of David would rescue his people from their distresses and subdue their enemies. He would purify Jerusalem and make it truly holy. His reign would produce conditions of peace such as the world had never known. To know something about the history of Israel, and about the strife and threats that Israel experienced within and from without, is to understand why the people would have embraced such a hope.

3 Among some Jews still today, the dream of a coming Davidic Messiah persists. When the prayer, the great *Shemoneh 'Esreh* (*The Eighteen Benedictions*), is prayed in synagogues, the fourteenth and fifteenth sections ask:

> *And to Jerusalem Thy city return with compassion, and dwell therein as Thou hast promised; and rebuild her speedily in our days, a structure everlasting; and the throne of David speedily establish therein. Blessed be Thou, O Lord, the builder of Jerusalem.*
>
> *The offspring of David Thy servant speedily cause to flourish, and let his horn be exalted in Thy salvation. For salvation do we hope daily. Blessed art Thou, O God, Who causest the horn of salvation to flourish.*

A HEAVENLY DELIVERER

1 In another line of thought, the Messianic Age would be ushered in directly by God, without any intermediary, Isaiah 64:1. No reference is made to a Messianic figure. This approach appears in Isaiah 24–27, 64:1, and in Haggai and Joel; see also Zephaniah 3:14–20.

2 This understanding occurs frequently in the Apocrypha and Pseudepigrapha, Baruch 4:21–37; Tobit 13:10–18; The Assumption of Moses 10:1–10; Jubilees 23:30–31. While the passages listed speak of the coming of the Messianic Age, the only actor in the drama is God. *God* will break into history *personally* and *directly*.

A HEAVENLY-HUMAN DELIVERER

1 A third pattern follows on from the second. Although the dream of the coming Messianic Age remained as vivid and persistent as ever, the possibility of its coming seemed to become more remote as each year passed. Freedom remained as distant as ever. Even in the Jews' brief days of liberty, anything even remotely resembling a world empire ruled by the Jews was not seen as a credible possibility. Moral degeneration and spiritual disenchantment prevailed increasingly in the national life. However, during this time the idea arose of a divine, superhuman Messiah who would break into history clad with the might of heaven, and who by superhuman means would establish what no human could bring about. With this development, the picture of the Messiah became a little more heavenly.

2 This hope found expression in two Jewish works of the first and second centuries B.C.

- In *Enoch*, the Messiah becomes a completely other-worldly figure of divine, majestic, and superhuman power, destined to conquer all and judge all, to obliterate sinners and exalt the righteous, 38:1,2; 45:3,4; 48:10; 49:2,4; 52:4.

- In *2 Esdras*, there are two pictures. In the *first*, the concept of a Davidic Messiah is combined with that of a divine, preexistent figure, 12:30–34. This one person is spoken of as the lion of Judah, who destroys the eagle (which is Rome).

The *second* picture speaks of the Messiah as *The Man from the Sea*.

> *After seven days I dreamed a dream in the night; and lo, a wind arose from the sea and stirred up all its waves. As I kept looking the wind made something like the figure of a man come up out of the heart of the sea. And I saw that this man flew with the clouds of heaven; and wherever he turned his face to look, everything under his gaze trembled, and whenever his voice issued from his mouth, all who heard his voice melted as wax melts when it feels the fire.* (2 Esdras 13:1–4)

The Most High has been keeping this Man from the Sea/Rider on the Clouds in His presence for many ages. When he finally comes, he needs neither spear nor shield. His opponents are obliterated by the power of his word, 2 Esdras 13:3,4, 21–56.

There is little resemblance between these hopes and the ministry of Jesus of Nazareth.

1 Many scribes and rabbis thought of the Messiah as one who would come to earth and then return to his glory. He would be a conqueror who would destroy many peoples and silence many kings. He would carry out a deliverance for God's people that could only be compared with the original Exodus and delivery from slavery in Egypt. He would bring a new law that would transcend the old law:

> *The law which man presently learns in this world is nothing in comparison with the Law of the Messiah.*

2 Furthermore, there were those who said that the Messiah had come but would not reveal his presence because of the sins of the people. Statements such as these were made:

> *If all Israel would together repent for one whole day, the redemption by the Messiah would follow.*

> *If Israel would keep only two Sabbaths as perfectly as they should be kept, then the Messiah would come.*

3 This explains why many Jews set out to obey the Law with passionate and even fanatical devotion. It also explains why many Jews looked on Jesus with such horror; He did not keep the strict demands of the Law. Worse, He seemed to them to be a hindrance to the coming of the Messiah. He often desecrated the Sabbath!

4 Some held that the Messiah had already been born as a child in Bethlehem, and that he was waiting in concealment—where, no one knew. However, he would suddenly emerge full-grown to begin governing his kingdom. In this context, note John 7:27 where the Jews argue that Jesus could not be the Messiah because they knew where He came from (Nazareth), but "when the Messiah comes, no one will know where he is from."

5 Although prior to Jesus' coming there was no consistent, cut-and-dried Messianic blueprint, a pattern does emerge. It is helpful to know something about this pattern in order to understand the reaction of the Jewish nation to the Messiah who finally came.

Events Before and After

BEFORE

1 Basic to Messianic hopes was the Jewish understanding of time. Jews divided time into two ages. There was this *present age*, which is wholly evil, under the dominion of Satan, and beyond all remedy. Then there was the *age to come*, the golden age of God.

2 The conviction grew that the first would not simply grow into the second within the natural flow of history, nor would the second come about through human action. The age to come would appear as a result of the direct intervention of God—with the breaking in of the Day of the Lord. It would be a day when the present order would be completely destroyed and a new heaven and a new earth divinely created.

3 The events preceding and following the Day of the Lord would be traumatic. Elijah would return to be the Messiah's herald and forerunner, Malachi 3:1; 4:5,6. The prophet would stand on the hills of Israel and announce the Messiah's coming with a voice so loud that it would be heard from one end of the world to the other. Some held that Elijah would settle all disputes and carry out a ministry of reconciliation among humanity, and lead the people into that great act of repentance without which the Messiah would not come. "Israel," it was said, "will not bring forth the great repentance before Elijah comes". Some said he would anoint the Messiah into office.

4 Many believed that when the Messiah came, the Gentile nations would experience agony, destruction, and terror, and that the New Age would be born out of these pangs, Isaiah 25–32. Some saw it as a time of universal upheaval (Joel 2:1,2; Zephaniah 1:14–16) during which horror would be piled on horror, Isaiah 13:10; Joel 2:30,31; 3:15.

5 The visions became more bizarre and fantastic, predicting not only the physical disintegration of the universe, but also the disintegration of all personal relationships. All friendship, loyalty, and love would be obliterated. At the beginning of the Messianic Age, a judgment would take place, Malachi 3:1–3; Isaiah 13:9–11; 24:21,22; 66:15,16.

AFTER

1 A prominent feature of the dreams associated with the Messianic Age was the ingathering of Israel. Throughout the centuries, the Jews had been scattered across the ancient Near East. Sometimes they had been forcibly removed from their own land. Sometimes they had gone by their own choice to seek the new opportunities other lands offered. However, when the Messiah finally came, all Jews would be gathered back to Israel—in particular, to Jerusalem, Isaiah 11:11,12; 27:12,13; Micah 7:11–17. Even the Gentiles and nature itself would do everything possible to help them make their way back, Isaiah 49:22,23; 66:20. Some believed that the kingdoms of Judah and Israel would be reunited, Jeremiah 3:18; Hosea 1:11; Ezekiel 37:15–23.

2 A central hope in relation to the coming Messianic Age was the vision of a restored and renewed Jerusalem. The city would be beautified and filled with the precious gifts all the world would bring to it, Isaiah 54:11,12; 60:4–7,11–13,16,17; Haggai 2:6–9.

3 Other hopes with regard to the coming age were:
   a. It would be a time of amazing fertility, Amos 9:13; Isaiah 32:15; 29:17; 35:1; Joel 3:18.

145

b. War and strife would end, and peace would prevail, Isaiah 2:4, 11:9; Micah 4:1–4; Zechariah 9:10.

c. Humans and animals would live together in peace, Isaiah 11:6–9; 65:25; Hosea 2:18. (See also Mark 1:13: Jesus was with the wild beasts, and they did not harm Him.)

d. All pain, weariness, and even death itself, would be no more, Jeremiah 31:13; Isaiah 25:7, 26:19, 33:24, 35:10, 65:20–22; Daniel 12:2,3.

e. The manna would fall from heaven again, 2 Baruch 29:8.

f. The dead would return to life, Isaiah 25:8; Daniel 12:2. The literature of the intertestamental period devoted considerable attention to this hope, Psalms of Solomon 3:16, 13:9–11, 15:13–15; 2 Maccabees 7:9,14,23; Testament of Judah 25:1–4; Enoch 51:1; 2 Esdras 13:32,37; Testament of Benjamin 10:8; 2 Baruch 30:1–5, 50:1–4, 51:6.

Jesus' actions in raising three people from the dead (Mark 5:21–24, 35–43; Luke 7:11–17; John 11:1–44) made a powerful statement. They declared that the Messianic Age had come, and that Jesus was and is the Messiah.